Koyopa: Contact Within

Koyopa: Contact Within

The Plumed Serpent Rises

Eileen Meyer

Edited by Monica Markley

Dedication

To Mother Earth and the Awakening Natural Human

Table of Contents

Acknowledgments

Eduardo, we have been blessed to spend time and work together in this life. Sometimes our paths took us in completely different directions, yet we always knew that the deeper spiritual work was far more important than the smaller scripts of the mundane world. Thank you for your timely encouragement and the shared experience of this Greater Love and purpose. Gratitude and appreciation to you, Robert Shapiro, for your unconditional and dedicated work for humanity and for lifting me up into the atmosphere of my authenticity. I have absolute respect for you, my friend, and for your immense, warm, and generous heart. To Maggie, my angel, thank you for seeing me and supporting my part in the greater plan. To Darryl Anka, thank you for drawing me into the truth of who I am all those years ago. Without your demonstrated courage to be you, I'm not sure I would've found the courage to be me. Thank you, James, for pressing me to see the gift and take that next big step. Many thanks to Monica Markley for your amazing editing skills, for being a loving witness to my story, and for recognizing the value of sharing it with the world. My son, I love you with all my heart. Your soul is an ancient one and therefore strong and able in helping others navigate these times. It is a joy to watch you share your heart's wisdom with all your relations. To my Father, I love you unconditionally. Larry Mitchell, your musical support and encouragement was endless. How wonderful to join you in the sweet creation of unexpected songs and sound. And to my good friend, Candida Jones, thank you for your synchronous magic in pointing me toward trauma therapy. This was a huge leap in my understanding of the energetics around trauma, the release of it, and opening to embody more of the Self. To Tomas and the Solace Crisis Treatment Center – my gratitude for your care and healing support at my time of need. You were key in helping me release the past, stabilize, and accelerate my work. To Lori, Steve, and the boys – it cannot be overstated – your love and friendship has kept me alive and afloat in this world, thank you. To Sue Ayers, your heart, help, and friendship (and quick turnaround with transcription) is so valued and appreciated. Corri, Brandon, and Mary – thank you for believing in me. To my family and the rest of my trusted friends throughout this journey, I'm grateful for your presence and influence in my life. I know that in relation to me, it hasn't always been easy, clear-cut, or straightforward. I thank you for keeping an open mind.

In 1984 – 1985, Dr. Peter Gariaev and his team of Russian linguists were studying DNA and the ways light, sound and frequencies interact with DNA. Their research led to many groundbreaking and paradigm-shifting discoveries with one of them showing that DNA is able to absorb and emit light (photons), which spirals along the double helix in sacred geometrical form. Literally, DNA creates magnetized wormholes in the space-time fabric. DNA acts as "tunnel connections between entirely different areas in the universe through which information can be transmitted outside of space and time. The DNA attracts these bits of information and passes them on to our consciousness." The researchers found that with the presence of light (photons), DNA activation and thus evolution can occur.[1]

~ Dr. Kathy J. Forti

Individuals capable of generating high ratios of heart coherence were able to alter DNA conformation according to their intention. Intending to denature (un-wind) or renature (wind) the DNA had corresponding effects on the UV spectra. As people learn to sustain heart-focused positive feeling states, the brain can be brought into entrainment with the heart. The conclusion is the need of pointing to the heart as the center of consciousness.[2]

~ DR. FAHAD BASHEER

Introduction

When I was three years old, I became obsessed with reading books – lots of them. By the time I was a first grader, the principal and my teacher placed me in a fifth-grade reading class. It seemed to resolve the issue of my fidgeting. In my reality, each book was a song. I loved the steady rhythm, music, and overtones of imagination that blossomed from each page. The Natural World was the same. I listened to the song, and I was the song – no separation. Life was magical that way, and I knew instinctively that my heart was about creating songs too.

Nearly five decades have passed, and here I am. I've written many songs in my life, but this is my first book. They became separate things somewhere along the way. I've had help with this lifelong book project. It's just one item on a kind of wish list from the angels. Early on, I started calling them angels because I liked the word, and the definition provided by my religious mother seemed to fit. The word matched the feeling of my other family – the beings of light who were always with me and who spoke to me through a kind of wordless language in my heart. They showed me that I was connected to them through feelings, and these feelings were connected to a network of beautifully colored spheres of light. I was visited repeatedly. They arrived in this light, and they wrapped me inside their beautiful songs. I needed this resonant foundation. I needed to remember their love. Otherwise, I would not survive.

They left for a time, and after years of worldly conditioning had laid claim to my essence, the scope of the visits changed. They initiated a sort of re-entrainment program – once again lifting me to the baseline of what is inherent and natural. How quickly I had forgotten. How quickly we all forget.

We are far more than what we think – with far more consciousness beyond the spectrum of what people like to call normal. It turns out that the evolution of consciousness requires us to first activate and then reorient to the rest of our natural design. I took the lifetime course. I needed to know how to teach or remind others about the forgotten song. The problem was, I kept forgetting too. Thankfully, of the many beautiful qualities of angels, patience is one.

There were brief spans, between jobs and the usual challenges of life, that I did my best to show up for the assignment – to capture multidimensionality in a book. Silly optimistic me. There was never enough time to sink into the deepest kind of truth, and from there, let the magic arrive. I knew that the words needed to be sent out like fireflies – to first catch your eye and later, perhaps, guide you back to the feeling memory that this story is really about you. It's about all of us. Over a dozen times, I dedicated myself to the task. I sat down to write – using whatever free time I had. I fiddled with chapters, titles, intros, and swearwords. In the end, though, it turns out the fireflies only wanted to rehearse.

I had to be back in the world – powering down all the best parts of me in order to fit – yet again – in the name of money and survival. It was not an ordinary life with ordinary states of consciousness. This dedicated review of my life and compilation for the book has taken a year. It includes pieces of my journals dating back to 1980, hundreds of audio recordings, my musical poetry, and the cellular memories of direct encounters with nonhuman intelligence. And it all comes together at this timing because of the unexpected arrival of resources. Life is funny that way.

This story doesn't appear to fit into any existing genre or category. For most of my life, I could not find a contextual framework or the cerebral building blocks to explain any of it without being perceived as strange, crazy, or even mentally ill. It's why many experiencers don't come forward. The dreaded judgment and knee-jerk shaming has always been predictable. It makes perfect sense to stay in hiding. Yet, we are emerging. Many of us are able to see very clearly now the dense reality that humanity has been unconsciously contained within. It's not possible to stay quiet and enabling anymore. Experiencers of all kinds are being awakened and activated for this important timing. I am just one of many.

Occasionally, I like to ask people why they think humanity only uses 10 percent of their brains' capacity. It turns out it's a tad more than that, but most people I talk with believe this or at least feel as if we're only utilizing a small portion of what's possible. Scientists say that 98.8 percent of our DNA falls in the noncoding, or junk category. It definitely begs the question: Why? Yet we quite easily give our power over to the ones (assigned experts within our established institutions) who seem to know why this is. Remember, they also live within and study fragments of reality that we have assumed are all there is. What I learned was that until we activate or actualize our natural state of wholeness, we will forever loop in a closed-circuit reality of limitations and misunderstandings. It is why we can be so easily manipulated and controlled through fear, and it's why we can't seem to snap out of what we have been told, or programmed, to believe and defend as truth.

Many of us have had defining moments of lucidity in our lives, but we learn to dismiss them quite easily. The mesmerizing scripts and stories seem to prevail in the end, and we quickly return to the known, or prearticulated, reality. Our programming says that anything beyond the known is crazy. We learn to make jokes about our anomalies and nervously laugh it off so that we can maintain our solid-citizen identity – the identity that wins love, money, and a variety of other accolades from the world. It turns out that the key to breaking the spell and activating the rest of our consciousness is incredibly simple. Or rather, it sounds simple. We snap out of it when we directly speak, feel, and know the Truth. Yes, Truth with a capital *T*.

You may be familiar with this idea in your religious literature: Ye shall know the truth, and the truth shall set ye free. I will not judge or disrespect others' religious choices, but I'm as far from organized religion as one can get. Still, I not only agree with that statement, I can demonstrate it. Anyone can – religious or not. All that is required is to feel and speak the truth – not other people's truths, but our own. It takes effort and courage to locate this truth and give it voice. Soon all that is based on a lie in your individual life will shatter, and all that is real will remain.

Following the successful practice of this, we embody and live Truth naturally – beyond the mechanics of thought. It is then that we can expand it into the "where two or more are gathered" platform to rapidly dissolve the collective spells out there – the ones connected to the worldly definitions of money, politics, and power. I will show you what I've remembered – through my life of adapting to and practicing these principles that came from my Visiting Intelligence beyond the known – about our universal value beyond this matrix. It's taken a lifetime for me. The angels say that once committed to your own awakening, it will take far less time for you.

It's clear to me now that human beings have been conditioned to create a tiny image of themselves to interface with this world. We've adapted to the smaller box and have forgotten the totality of how gifted and expansive we are. We are incredible beings – naturally provided with far more capacity to see, know, and commune beyond the container of our world than we realize. We don't require rockets or spaceships to experience contact with extraterrestrial or nonhuman intelligence. In fact, it requires no special schooling. Nor does it require billions of dollars for research and equipment to talk to them via radio signals.

There's another message from the Bible: The Kingdom of Heaven is within. It turns out this is absolutely true too – but in a far more expansive way than religion or even mainstream science may have the awareness and heart aptitude to address. You have a huge power and network within you that lies dormant and requires present attention to awaken.

The early 1990s is when I decided that I was a contactee-experiencer – those who have had peak, lucid interactions with nonhuman intelligence. Before this, I wasn't concerned with being labeled by the world because I wasn't speaking out loud about it. Some of the given definitions applied to me, but not all. From what I have read in decades-old books and observed online, a great number of these contactees claim to have been abducted against their will. With this type of phenomenon, we often find the suggestion that our government is either hiding or participating in these events. I cannot, nor am I qualified to, speak to these scenarios. I have never felt abducted against my will. This does not mean that I didn't experience fear. There are others, like myself, who are aware that we previously agreed to a sort of cosmic contact program – established from a soul level or multidimensional (natural) state of being.

For me it has taken a lifetime to understand and process the fear that transforms into Love and to embody what I share with you here. None of it appears to make sense to the fragmented human consciousness – whatever the contact scenario. It seems that there are many who analyze and produce theories about this phenomenon, but why just entertain speculation from those who haven't had the actual experience? This will always be problematic, as contactees will tell you that there are multidimensional, sensory understandings that manifest through the actual encounter. These direct experiences cannot be fully or accurately defined within the smaller spectrum. It's probably why I was taught – or re-minded – how to translate frequency.

It seems that the human mind gets agitated with the unexplained – new data that doesn't fit nicely into the past foundation of what has always been. I was shown by this intelligence that nothing from the past will sufficiently explain it, but rising above the usual chatter and adapting to the resonant frequencies will naturally fill in the blanks – here in this natural state. We do not theorize. We know. IT will inform you of the truth inside every cell of your body. IT can do this because IT is your Source.

Personally, I am only interested in this ongoing ET conversation if it is oriented toward the transformation and evolution of human consciousness. This is what my life of being an experiencer seemed to revolve around – assisting me in activating more of my built-in hardware, as well as related upgrades in software, if you will.

My Visitors were highly evolved and extraordinarily loving. Sometimes they appeared in the form of tall, wispy, angelic-looking beings. Other times, they had the appearance of five-foot-tall humanoid Grays. On rare occasions, I would have telepathic dialogs with a gold-light, praying-mantis-looking being. While I find all these life forms fascinating, in all cases, there were no outer forms at all – none in the 3D variety, that is. The imagery always presented in the center of my mind's eye – in visions, lucid dreams, and altered states. My visits, and subsequent data downloads primarily revolved around communion through very high-vibratory, resonant frequency. The Visitor's written language forms and streams of odd-looking multidimensional symbols were incidental, and most times, they were completely irrelevant. It was the transfer of information through my heart and through the frequency of pure love and truth that was of the highest value to me.

All Visitors seemed to be onboard with an agenda to wake me up and out of my limited, worldly conditioning. Many times the high frequencies would initiate kundalini-type events, or the Mayan term, *Koyopa*. It seemed my physical body was not only included in these activities but essential for adapting to the frequencies and awakening into its supporting role. The purpose was always understood through the energy – to accelerate my consciousness into a greater sense of Self and objective here. Soon enough, I realized that there were many of us here – those who have had similar contact and wake-up-now protocols. Knowing this makes it far easier to proceed.

While I have trouble coming up with new adjectives for the Immense Love that I was introduced to, I still experienced many cycles of transcending fear while integrating the experience and then resting on neutral plateaus – until it all started again. I almost always felt afraid at the onset of a new phase of contact with them, but over time, I adapted. I would remember how to rebalance from the extremes in frequency and return to the understanding that, in the end, these visits were proven to be benevolent and empowering. My Visitors pointed out that the fear erupts through the contrast between our mundane, worldly vibration and their cosmic waves of exquisite energy. I understood that I was being stretched, and this chasm needed to be bridged before I could even begin to comprehend them or later learn to translate the encoded vibratory fields they arrived in.

At certain stages in this lifetime schedule, I would snap out of my conditioned mindset long enough to be present and apply what they had taught me. The tools and practice always revolved around initiating more of my available consciousness through a vibrational heart grid. It was then that I was restored to a more holistic understanding of life, along with ecstatic states of pure love. The heart grid is a natural grid that is connected to the Earth and beyond. It seems there is another grid, one that we have been contained within. It is a programmed one that we believed to be real, so we adapted to it and called it life. For a time, our conditioning to be small worked very, very well for the architects of this highly specific design. Actually, I refer to it now as a genius program of captivity and control, but it's not one that I consciously choose. I know better now. Soon we all will.

You'll find that I borrow a few terms from religion as well as science from time to time. Some terms I avoid altogether because they are highly charged with rigid connotation. "God" is one of these words. Believe me, I know beyond a shadow of a doubt that a Source Creator exists, but the word "God" doesn't lend itself to the direct-feeling landscapes of high-vibratory consciousness. I also make up my own terms because I'm either unaware that there is a word to describe the experience or mostly because there is no word. Of course I use analogy and metaphor to help describe the indescribable. Just imagine that I'm an explorer. I've been taken out of our limited container of consciousness so many times that I now feel more oriented to the landscapes of resonance, direct knowing, and unconditional love. For decades, I've wanted to share all of this, but I was busy surviving in this world like the rest of you. Money is the primary glue that keeps many of us stuck in loops of fear and forgetfulness. Rediscovering our inherent value within sets us on a path to freedom – actual freedom.

We all needed to reach this timing, whereby increasing populations are seeing with their own eyes first – that this experiment in smallness is over. Knowing thyself, thy heart, and thy truth is all-important now. Images and identities that were created for the sole purpose of interfacing with and surviving in the unreal world will dissolve. The sinner identity is pure fabrication. You are already forgiven because there is nothing to forgive. You are wholly loved, yet this Universal Love is pressing us to fully remember who we are, what we were designed to be, and to practice this in our world – right where we are. Not many can deny that the old reality is crashing down all around us. Time to wake up to all that is possible! We're perched on the threshold of the greatest new beginning we can barely imagine.

My Visitors reached me through a vast field of loving energy presence. It's the language of resonance. I now reach out to you through my life story as well as through frequency messages that I learned (or somehow already knew) how to decode. I still don't understand how it works, but I can share with you what they taught me about adapting to Source frequency, becoming whole again, and meeting the rest of our Selves and our greater communities.

I believe that other contactees would agree that by no means are we complete with the understanding and integration of these evolutionary, beyond space-time meetings. Yet at this stage, we may be a good support system for the future awakening of others. To achieve this, we make the individual choice to be more visible. Just as in other forms of "coming out" in our world, I'm quite sure there will be family members, friends, and communities who will judge and reject what I share. Still, my heart wants to do this. As grateful as I am for the angelic presence and guidance I've had throughout my life, I used to beg to have support from a human angel – with skin on. Someone who's been *here* too and could help me adapt to these extraordinary states of consciousness from the ground up.

My intent is to better prepare you for your own inner journey – into the high-vibrational center of your heart and being. Or maybe I'm completely crazy, and you shouldn't listen to me at all. The bottom line is this is me – being honest and vulnerable. It's a simple offering – a few stories, a scratched-out roadmap, some tools, and heartfelt good wishes as you set out on your own pilgrimage to Self and Source. In addition, I have included some of my own epiphanies, engaging my heart-based instincts to connect the dots around the Mayan Calendar, 2012, and how it relates to us in present time. Trust me, if it unfolds in the way that I've been shown repeatedly throughout my life, soon you'll find these evolutionary changes to be the most real and present thing in your life too. After many transcendent excursions, I am absolutely convinced that we are transforming to our whole and natural state first. Following restoration, we can celebrate the simple joys of remembering who we are and feel in actual terms the power and beauty of the Universal Song that we are all connected to.

Imagine that – a world that directly reflects and resonates our true selves, not just another image but rather our whole and actualized Selves on Earth. My sincerest thanks for opening your minds and hearts to my story – our story – and the full remembrance of *our song*.

I

Bridging
From Mechanics to Resonance

———✸———

*... Or perhaps some will hold out to play
the "hundredth monkey" role.
In this case, they would simply lose their grip
from the monkey bars when the
sufficiently enlightened collective creates the
morphogenetic field that literally pulls
them out of their mechanized past.[3]*

~ Dr. Rupert Sheldrake

They were just as normal to me as my bucket, my shovel, and my sand-filled shorts. We would converse for hours in the sandbox on the north side of the house about things I couldn't have known or spoken of as a child. Sometimes I recall talking out loud, but mostly I just knew what they were sharing, or communing, with me via the feelings, tones, and moving pictures that played in my mind's eye. Everything was fine and dandy until I told my mom how much I loved the tall blue and gold people. They were bright, and they looked a little like the pictures of angels I'd seen depicted in books and on TV – soft, wispy shapes of light. They did not have wings, yet to me they were my angel family, who visited me in the sandbox, in my bedroom at night, and down by the creek where I merged with the trees, the birds, and the pollywogs. I was still an innocent who had not yet disconnected from her natural state. In this vivid reality, I had many delightful friends, including three beautiful horses, that followed me everywhere – to the grocery store, when I walked to school, and even on our family vacations. I remember feeling safe and comforted by their presence, imaginary or not. My mother wasn't comforted by any of it.

It took a long time to adjust to living in the world. Actually, I'm not sure I've ever fully achieved that. The little blonde tomboy and her wild imagination was tolerated for a while, but soon I was being asked by my parents and schoolmates to, "Stop with the crazy stories!" So I did. But only after my loving, otherworldly friends did their best to explain. I was informed through their distinct spheres of harmonic messages that my imagination and my ability to perceive them would be leaving me for a while. Sure enough, the white, brown, and black trio of horses disappeared shortly thereafter. Try as I might, I could not conjure them up again. I remember crying for many nights until I simply grew tired of being sad. Yet I remained in full trust that one day I would reconnect with them – my real family – again. Alas, it seems that as my body grew bigger, the sound and creative expression of my spirit grew much, much smaller – inaudible and invisible, you might say. Conditioning does that.

Thankfully, in my early teen years this Intelligence returned; however, it was a bittersweet reunion. During the visits, I felt a polarizing joy and enormous pain all at once. In the cosmic direction, I was in the full embrace of Pure Vibratory Love, and it felt like it was the Source of All reaching out to know me. However, in the worldly direction – that is, my everyday life with everyday responsibilities – I was now hyper-aware of the growing contrast this generated within my conditioned psyche. It turns out it's quite difficult to keep up with 3D protocols following the direct and felt experience of a near-unbearable level of Cosmic Love in the body. It had to remain a secret, though, because that was crazy talk in the world out there. It also presented a fascinating conundrum to me: The spiritual community not only seemed to have no interest (no matter the religion or belief system) but the subject also clearly made them uncomfortable and sometimes even angry to hear of it. It seems there was no one in my life at the time, or for decades to come, who could relate to me or simply support me in reconciling everyday life to these epic doses of Love.

When it was discussed, it seemed that most could not move past the cognitive dissonance that occurred without the pre-approved, religious, or scientific framework to comfort the gatekeeper of the mind. In my experience, the direct feeling of Creation naturally contains all that the individual needs to know from within the Self. When I was a child, this was already integrated and functioning. I would never have thought to compare or question it. The conditioning had not yet "dis-integrated" my natural consciousness.

During my adult years, the repetitive nature of these visits helped me to adapt to consistently expanding frequencies, which naturally reoriented me to the streaming, heart-based consciousness once again. I had to be reminded of what this natural state of being felt like and how it worked, as well as learn through frequency messages that every human being is designed for this. However, our conditioning into valuing and engaging only a limited area of our consciousness removes us from the present, and our inner communion capacities are subsequently knocked offline.

All this contact occurs in the present moment. Framing it into language to one who does not feel it removes it from the present moment. Also, searching outside to find an explanation, validation, or symbolic comparison with what already exists out there to what actually occurred here, again, removes it from the present moment. All these scenarios have a tendency to take us to the past, a place where we can be thrown off-balance and outside of our own center of power and knowing. This offline way of life caused us to look to others who wear suits, robes, or lab coats as the authorities that help us to fill in all the missing pieces here. Frankly, we have all been fragments of consciousness looking to authority or others out there to complete us. Soon, as more and more initiate the rest of their natural operating system within, we will be amazed that we were ever able to live and function under such extremely limiting circumstances.

Through the variety of peak experiences in my life, I am now aware that human consciousness has entered an evolutionary intersection. There is a natural doorway within to meet, know, and resonate with our Source directly. I discovered this doorway before I had the terminology for it from the world. The experiences were pure, real, and wordless. Later I learned that the Sanskrit term for this restoration is Kundalini. The Maya described it as Koyopa. I believe that these openings have always been available to us, but at the galactic-cycle timing prophesied by the Maya and a myriad of other ancient peoples, it becomes far more available. It is perceivable not because an authority in the outer world told us so, but because we can now choose to engage with it and directly feel it in our hearts and physical forms.

Generally, we have been conditioned to adapt into a primarily left-brained, patriarchal reality. It was nearly impossible for us to know any different. After centuries of building lives, cultures, and identities from this one-sided, fragmented consciousness, we have arrived into our twenty-first century of increasing insanity, disease, and irrefutable chaos. Many of us can be heard muttering under our breath, "This just can't go on."

The question is quite clear: Is this what we want? That depends. The answer, it turns out, needs to come from the individual and from within. It's personal but not deeply so until one is exposed to an actual vibrational experience, or meet-your-maker event. Whatever the event – near-death experiences (NDEs) or contact with ETs or related spirit phenomenon – it is a direct experience of a greater reality, whereby we are fundamentally changed. In most cases, after exposure to more, we are dropped back into the smaller reality. When the peak experiencer's worldview and related 3D identities are obliterated, our answers to these existential questions will be very different. Through the contrast, one becomes ultra-aware of the more limited way of life that we once thought was so real. Is this life? Is this what being human is? I can tell you very clearly what my answer is – no.

Experience changes everything. I choose differently now because I *know* that there is more.

I've been shown that humanity is standing in the center of two major choices now: Stay with the conditioning that we are small, unsafe, worthless, and powerless and that we will not survive without the architects of our world telling us who we are, how to feel, or what to do at any given moment. Otherwise, we commit to rebooting our Natural State and our natural-intelligence network. In this feeling-remembrance, we ignite and fully awaken the heart consciousness as well as our natural, inner technologies that link us to this greater Field of Intelligence.

Is it possible for us to remember our natural state again? How do we collectively re-access the right brain – the feminine – and the rest of our consciousness when a significant number of people appear to be unaware that anything is missing? Our hearts and every cell in every body are specifically designed to help. From my own experience of standing in this all-important intersection, I found there was a prerequisite: feel. Allow the feminine aspects of your being to be restored. Adapt to the present, and let go of all that you thought you knew from the past. This may sound like a massive undertaking, I know. But as I stepped into the mindfulness of my Visitor's recommended practices, I found it to be quite freeing and utterly glorious – when I was all by myself, that is. No matter the level of mind-blowing, ecstatic communion and the resulting expansion of consciousness, the paradox remained. We're all doing this together.

Throughout my life, when I found it necessary to blend back into the more limiting agreements of the past – for employment, in relationships, in family life, and so forth – I found it mostly to be a drain and detriment to my own growing sense of aliveness. Yet out of necessity, I would subsequently begin chopping away the parts of myself that didn't fit, made people uncomfortable, or couldn't be easily explained. As you may know, in the smaller bandwidth of consciousness, it is important to appear normal. I wasn't very successful with this routine, as it eventually made me ill, depressed, and anxious. Sound familiar? The American statistics are alarming. Millions upon millions of people suffer from addictions, anxiety, and depression-related disease. And the numbers only grow. I believe our collective soul is trying to get our attention to remind us that there is so much more to the story. The outer world had always informed me that this was "just the way it is." Have a drink. Take a pill. Again, no thank you. I don't accept this limited, problem-solution cycle anymore.

The lifetime schedule with this loving intelligence was intense. The Love seemed to arrive in planned gradations of pure energy. Sometimes it arrived in the forms of the tall angel beings. Other times it morphed into praying-mantis-looking beings. Many times, when I was receiving healings, surgeries, or even giving birth to a hybrid baby, it was the tall, fuzzy-faced (or veiled) Grays. But always, no matter the presenting form, it was intelligent frequency that spoke to me from within. Some call it telepathy. At times, it seemed to reverberate inside my head, but mostly it spoke to me inside my entire body. All these forms would interact with me for healings, teachings, and dialogs, but the overall agenda revolved around assisting me – on all levels – to acclimate to a higher frequency.

After a certain plateau was achieved, it shifted. The teaching then revolved around how to initiate a connection and communion with them – to practice accessing more of my consciousness and abilities. It came through ET visits as well as repeated Koyopa, bioenergetic events. Sometimes my Visitors would set off the transformational, body-centered episodes, and other times it would unfold more specifically through an inner coaching that felt impossible to translate into words.

I would try to explain it to others – the altered states that felt far more real than our everyday kind of real. But when I tried to describe the resonant methods in which the data arrived, for the most part, I just sounded like a blithering idiot. It was best to keep it inside – literally inside my cells – until there was a clear recipe and a visible container in which to serve it up for human cognition. The one constant throughout these interactions was a high pitch of vibrational energy, so high that many times I would have to cry out, "Stop! This... is... too much. *Please.*" And they would stop, until the next time, that is.

Every time I found myself doubting my sanity or wanting to give up on what felt like their pressing, otherworldly plan, I would experience a powerful lucid dream or visitation with the Presence. It was always the tone or feeling of the connection that would "re-mind" and restore me to what the original intent for contact was all about. No words. Pure resonance delivered instantaneous healing and understanding that it was about reconnecting with Source, where there is no us and them. I would become lucidly aware that I was equal with my Visitors and one with our Loving Source. I felt as if I were living, playing, and exploring within these infinite fields of possibility. It was there that I found the resolve to go on despite the fact that I still had no concrete reflection of this in my outer world.

It is my understanding that if I ever truly wanted it to stop, it would have. This communication through resonance was initiated in childhood. It was natural to me, but it didn't take long to learn that other kids, even my own family, did things very differently. I became an observer mostly – watching everyone adapt and conform to all that was solid and visible in their spectrum. I suppose if I too had climbed onto the monkey-bar matrix and identified only with it, I would've been like most people and had a more normal life. Instead, I kept to myself, and the lessons from the Intelligence continued.

I learned patience, perseverance, trust, and present-moment living. Throughout my life, I remained the invisible little girl on the playground, on the sidelines sitting in the sand and always wondering why playing on the monkey bars was the singular object of attention here. Do these bars symbolize the small percentage of what we are supposedly using of our brains and DNA? To me, there was clearly an infinite field of information, magic, and play that was hiding in plain sight – or should I say, hiding in plain feeling? I saw and felt far more in the spaces between the monkey bars, but I learned quickly that it wasn't welcome here. It wasn't discussed.

On the flip side, there were also times that I pleaded for this elusive normalcy. I screamed at them, my Visitors, from the rubble of my repeated collapse: "Why me?" I was certain there had to be far more suitable human resources to work with than I, whatever the overall goal might be. I was intelligent, but I had trouble learning what I was supposed to learn here and securing a foothold in the existing infrastructure. Very little appealed to me in the way of life choices here.

I was convinced that my Visitors were wrong in choosing me. This imagined purpose, this expanded communication project, this design to remind, whatever it was, would just not be possible. How do I draw from the light data inside my cells and translate it into a word language? No one could ever tell me how to do that. I tried to channel or become a medium for it, but the methodology wasn't quite right. The Intelligence within said, "No, this isn't exactly how we're going to do it. You have the right idea to translate, but we're building a new roadmap." Later, it just happened – by locking into a resonant communion while messages flowed through me – and I gave it voice in words, in real time. That was pretty cool, but soon I realized that this form was far too small for the massive amounts of multidimensional data that streamed in. It clearly preferred to be known and valued in a wordless way.

While I cherish the hundreds of messages that I have brought through, and continue to bring through, I felt it was far more efficient to help other humans remember how to directly commune with this greater intelligence. It no longer matters what terms we use – channeling, communion, or what have you – as these methods are temporary. In our natural state, there is no need for language or translation. In fact, words can even be a hindrance.

In these times, the direct and sustained experience of Love seems to be a foreign concept to most. Angels, ecstatic experiences, and "knowings" were for Bible characters and church-designated saints. I didn't have the right gender, age, looks, or even an affiliated institution to cast me as a viable spiritual or philosophical voice here. Still, ever since I can remember, I've had an unexplained inner drive to report to other human beings that there was another whole way of being human. They needed to know that they could bypass the smaller narrative here and go directly to it. I had to let them know that their God, or the Creator of All, was not just an idea or concept but rather a felt experience that danced within every cell of their bodies.

I, or We, reach out in this form for the purpose of building bridges – from a local, linear approach that utilizes language – to a more spherical, non-local connection that I refer to as communion. The latter method is not contained or defined within time and space. It is instantaneous knowing. Therefore, it's like having a quantum, beyond-local telephone plan that we simply forgot we had.

> *Once we accept quantum nonlocality as an established*
> *physical aspect of the world in which we live,*
> *it becomes easier within science to conceive of a*
> *transcendent domain outside the manifest*
> *physical domain of space-time.*[4]

~ DR. AMIT GOSWAMI

I will do my best in the following chapters to take you through some of my more memorable, radically transformative experiences as well as provide a portion of the wisdom delivered through my contact. However, I refuse to pick just one existing label for this phenomenon so that our minds can bypass the anxiety of not having a pigeonhole. Minds are like that, you know. Does "angel" feel like the right word? Archangels? Saints? Jesus? Buddha? How about God or Goddess? Higher Self? Or maybe ET works best for you. I use all of these terms and more, simply because I'm trying to connect with you, and these are some of the labels drawn out from our collective pool of shared spiritual-authority words and symbols. If it helps you to let down your guard and welcome who or what is being shared here, I encourage you to choose or identify with the loving being, or beings, that best represent spiritual authority for you. That is, until you recognize that the spiritual authority is actually you, or you actualized.

Language and linear thought has been our primary mode and system of communication here. We adapted to it well, but I discovered through resonant contact that it isn't our wholly, natural way. It seems that humanity has always been wired for these long-distance (or beyond-local) calls. We simply haven't been informed that it is so. Instead of accessing our very sophisticated technologies within, we were conditioned to build smaller, 3D identities and earn a living instead of knowing our value and actually living. Human beings are designed to be one of the finest adaptive life forms in this entire cosmic creation. It's just what we do. Evidence of this in our 3D lives is undeniable, but most of our triumphant stories of adaptation here have been in the direction of extreme limitation and contraction. Today we are shifting from this direction. We are now standing on the threshold of attuning to our whole and natural state, where all of our human courage, resourcefulness, and ingenuity are instead applied to the extremes of rapidly expanding consciousness.

This is about our evolution – returning to our natural state and more. But how do we evolve when the feminine (right brain) aspect of our consciousness is still quite ignored or invisible here? The feminine is the soul, the instinct, the spaces in between, the living waters, and the feeling-knowing data that has been conditioned out of us and ultimately devalued here in our modern human cultures. I'm not an expert in reporting the ancient, mythical stories concerning the return of the feminine. For me, it's simply about allowing the invisible portions of our consciousness and capacities to manifest once again so that we can reclaim the inheritance of our whole power – no matter the gender or pronoun we identify with.

We have been heavily programmed to see only a portion of reality. And now we stand at the crossroads of employing artificial intelligence (AI) and advanced technologies to enhance our brains. Don't get me wrong, I enjoy technology. However, my question is, "Do we want to engage and implement transhumanist technologies before we even understand how to access and synthesize the greater part of our own natural consciousness? In fact, the Visitors have really pressed this into me. AI can only attempt to copy or mirror the extremely advanced technologies that we already contain within. Perhaps this will be something to ponder before saying yes to what appears to be the perfect solution, or *fix,* for our so-called limited brain capacity. In my opinion, the enhancement of fragments of consciousness would take us into an entirely different trajectory of existence – perhaps even a dangerous one. From my viewpoint, taking responsibility for bringing our own natural state and capacities back online is a far more interesting, empowering, and exciting choice.

My conundrum has been how to share feeling data from my lifelong laboratory of direct experience. It's actual, and of course, it's subjective. Meeting your maker is as subjective as it gets. It's the marriage of the masculine and feminine within. It's a celebration of Absolute Love. It's Self-awareness. Most humans aren't even aware that they are programmed to *not* feel or perceive it. In fact, they are programmed to suppress feelings within themselves and to judge them as weaknesses when they surface in others. Ironically, I found that conscious feelings become the proverbial breadcrumbs – leading us *through* limitation and back to our full connectivity with the Whole of Creation.

One of the most important stages in my ongoing reorientation to wholeness was recovery from the past. I had to get help to heal the traumas that occurred throughout my life – in the form of molestation, sexual assault, domestic violence, and bullying – simply for being different. The wounds lay dormant within me, and my victim self would be triggered when I was near my abusers or when I was around the same feelings or vibration of violence. The reminders would erupt and demand attention through the only language it knew – depression, panic, and anxiety. I was informed by my Visitors, through their singing language, or cellular resonance, that I would not go further with this restoration protocol until every trauma was acknowledged, released, and completely healed. The residue from trauma (as well as poor nutrition, substance abuse, and so on) prevents the more sustained, resonant connection that bridges to our whole, nonlocal consciousness. Glimpses may occur, as we have referred to in the past framing of peak or mystical experience, but the uninterrupted, fully synchronized Oneness with our Source is ours when we commit to the conscious work.

When my anxiety attacks could no longer be ignored, a psychotherapist friend pointed me in the direction of EMDR[5] and Brain Spotting[6] trauma-therapy modalities. EMDR (Eye Movement Desensitization and Reprocessing) is a psychotherapy that enables people to heal from the symptoms and emotional distress that are the result of disturbing life experiences. Repeated studies show that by using EMDR therapy people can experience the benefits of psychotherapy that once took years to make a difference. It is widely assumed that severe emotional pain requires a long time to heal. EMDR therapy shows that the mind can in fact heal from psychological trauma much as the body recovers from physical trauma.[7]

Brainspotting is a powerful, focused treatment method that works by identifying, processing, and releasing core neurophysiological sources of emotional/body pain, trauma, dissociation and a variety of other challenging symptoms. Brainspotting is a simultaneous form of diagnosis and treatment enhanced with Biolateral sound, which is deep, direct, and powerful yet focused and containing.[6]

I found these modalities to be easy, fast, and highly effective in purging what I call, "trauma goo." Following this, I was immediately present, and I was able to accommodate increasing levels of resonant light and sound within my body. There are many energy-psychology, trauma-therapy modalities that can assist and even jumpstart our evolution forward into wholeness. Our hearts will lead us to the facilitators who can best serve our needs and in the right timing for us.

Once we are clear and back online, resonance receives the call and initiates the overtones of our greater selves. It is both natural and simple – almost too simple. Therein lies the challenge for most who are conditioned to emphasize and value only the thinking mind while suppressing and distorting their feeling-knowing capacities. We're absolutely wired to access more through a heart-based network and language that we have been encouraged to ignore throughout our lives. Still, the sweetness that is ours cannot be fully heard under the din of our addiction or the agreement to stay small. We must consciously choose to rise up and out.

Over the years, I listened to the suggestions and applied what came through this resonant language. I began calling it the Gold-Light Intelligence. It pressed me to consciously challenge all that was not representative of my true nature along with related personas and revenue streams. So I did. The results were extraordinary and life enhancing. Then there was everybody else – out there – in my community and my world. "How do I actually be more of who I am – out there?" I noticed that when I set aside what I knew to be true and assumed these worldly masks, I was also enabling those around me to continue pretending that this everyday reality is all that we have to work with. This hypnotic, unconscious behavior leaves us prone to forgetting and falling into the addiction of small thinking – again and again. Our courage to be present and authentic within our own individual consciousness is a key part of the mass-awakening equation. We must be bold enough to be it in the world. Gone are the spiritual teachers we once tucked away in caves and placed up on pedestals. Indeed, they have inspired us. But today we all have the opportunity to be spiritual demonstrators – resonating with Love, rejoining the timeless fluid that all Natural Beings are made of and swim within.

Many of us may be feeling alone and confused in a sort of purgatorial limbo, knowing intuitively that a transition can be made to this larger sense of Self and to a greater heart consciousness and community. Unfortunately, it appears that there is no clear, linear path from the past to this collective future. So we remain frozen – at the foot of the great wall of paradox.

Following repeated exposure to this high-vibratory contact, the only refuge and inspiration that I received from my outer world were the great outdoors – the natural world. Otherwise, it was nearly impossible to find a reflection of this Unconditional Love in my day-to-day existence. How would I explain the availability of this expansion and ecstasy of Source Love to others? How could I speak authoritatively of the timeless visits, the full-body orgasmic arching and contorting fits synced in resonance with Pure Love? I was still handicapped with a cultural identity that lacked in worldly credentials and titles that other humans were conditioned to expect. Who could I share this with, the wisdom that seemed to light up and sing to every cell in my body, the many journeys and the ensuing integration of new and greater landscapes of consciousness? Certainly not anyone indoctrinated into religion or science. Seriously, what did I know? Even if I could articulate it, why should anyone in the world listen to me? I couldn't even finish college. Life circumstances forced me out of my traditional education numerous times. Thankfully, I found resonant markers and encouragement from the ancient Earth-wisdom teachings that could still be accessed in the outer world. It was enough to keep me balanced and sane through what oftentimes felt like too fast and far too many expansion episodes for one human girl.

Over time, this contact with more of my Self radically changed me. Every existing title or career definition here felt excruciatingly small. My natural way of being and perceiving caused me to gravitate to the existing realms of music and poetry, but I never fully found my place there either. I confounded my family and many friends along the way. In their view, with my vocal talent, I could've easily been famous or successful. I don't know about that. However, what I do know – by heart and by direct experience – is a lot about who we are and what we're naturally connected to. It's beyond amazing and beyond words. And through feeling-frequency, it is totally knowable by all. To me, this is a far more interesting and rewarding line of work and service: to help my community recall the Truth inside that sets them free.

I know it's coming, this evolutionary leap from mechanized thinking into whole, resonant knowing – the full reconciliation and balance of the masculine and feminine within each of us. I feel it in my blood and my bones. And I saw it in a movie in the center of my mind's eye. It was repeated many times by the angel beings who stood at the perimeter of my childhood sandbox.

Thankfully, there is evidence that we are waking up and out of this disempowering, polarizing reality, where it seems we were ripe and quite easily plucked for control and manipulation. It's over now. I don't care about the who, what, why, where, and when of the past. It's a waste of energy. I'm all about now – where the birth of what's next is no longer dictated by outer conditioning and patriarchal authority but rather facilitated through natural, instinctual, and passionate states. It is here that our power is reclaimed. It is a power that lies not in the distant heavens, not in the distant future, and not in the past (when everything was supposedly better) but here and now, in our bodies, and on the present ground of planet Earth.

Quite often over my lifetime, my lessons about the practice of resonance or sound were always delivered with a highly magnetic, strongly feminine feeling. Then there was the coloring of gold – not just an outer coloring of gold-white light, but also the message and feeling that we *are* gold light. It feels like a crossroads – a cycle of opportunity for all to reactivate these shades and elements into our perceptible spectrum of awareness again. Matching myself to the feeling and color of this gold frequency is how I am able to hear the music and render into song – both as a songwriter and as a resonant-wisdom translator. I was taught from within how to talk or sing myself into the vibration of what I know as Source frequency – aka Love, Truth, and Light. I know instantly when I am in harmonic resonance with IT. It is then that I do not identify as Source, nor am I identified as the receiver. Instead, I am fully bridged and one with All – linked through resonant spheres of Love. This is *our* natural state.

...It is like an object coming from the unconscious with a compensatory function - to turn us away from the rational and toward the intuitive; to turn us away from the paternalistic, Apollonian, solar, masculine view of things, and toward a kind of watery, lunar, mysterious, intuitively felt feminine force – almost as though the UFO is a manifestation of Gaia as mother goddess. Science, as the proudest (pardon the word) erection of the rational mind, then is challenged by something from an entirely other dimension, an entirely other realm, that concretizes for us the culture crisis. And that's why I've gotten into UFOs; I think they are important for a resolution of the culture crisis. They concretize the struggle between the paternalistic-masculine and the lunar-feminine, between a dominator society and the kind of partnership society that we require to survive. [8]

~ TERENCE MCKENNA

II

What Do I Know?
Feeling My Way Through Life

—⚬⚬⚬—

But instinct is something which transcends knowledge. We have, undoubtedly, certain finer fibers that enable us to perceive truths when logical deduction, or any other willful effort of the brain, is futile.

~ NIKOLA TESLA

As an innocent child, I applied resonance as a natural way to connect with my angel friends and to always know what I needed to know. It was easy. Like most, in the first few years of my life, my family and community granted me permission to be a child – essentially freeing me to engage with my fantastical imagination. As I grew older, I was told by virtually everyone that it was the wrong way and that it wouldn't work in the world. Later, I would develop learning disabilities, a speech impediment, and experience indescribable fears of being seen or spoken to. I was confused and off-balance most of the time, but I did my best to figure out the bizarre rules of the game here. In school and related social activities, all I wanted was to be invisible and blend into the plain-beige background of life.

One thing that I am sure of is that I don't really know anything here, in the world. Finally, in my fifth decade of life, I understand the wisdom of this detached way of being now. It seemed that my entire life followed a certain natural modus operandi (MO) that was founded in, "Don't get too attached to anything here. Stay neutral, and 'tune into' the Truth that permeates all." I know that this may sound nebulous, but it was an inner guideline that always made perfect sense to me. Thankfully, I'm still here. What I mean by that is I'm not dead or institutionalized like I know others – other *peak* experiencers like me – might be.

My anchor was to always stay with the frequency throughout these transformational episodes: "Don't think. Trust the *feeling* of Love." This was the constant – the one message – that was communicated every time by the Intelligence as it swirled with light, sound, passion, and conviction throughout my body. I would've gone mad without that all-important message, as it seemed there was no stopping this preordained evolutionary program. While I didn't get the advance memo for this universal course, the frequency spoke to me every time. I was remembering how to hear and comprehend this language that danced and sang to me from within.

> *peak experience*
> *noun, Psychology.*
> *1. a high point in the life of a self-actualizer, during which the person feels ecstatic and more alive and whole than is usual.*[9]

Apparently, word got out that I was open. The peak experiences throughout my life involved angels, ETs, archetypes, animal spirits, fairies, and more. Still, I found that meeting all these colorful characters along the way was not a destination but rather part of a journey, one that prepared me to meet the ultimate – my Greater Self that knew its Source. Still, this clarity or whole view became more fleeting and sporadic over the years. Mostly, it would make for a very challenging life of repeating cycles of expansion and contraction. I would remember and forget, remember and forget. These other forms of intelligence showed up to help through the songs, or language of the heart. It was glorious and life-enhancing. Still, the more they showed up, the more different, or abnormal, I became.

Growing up, and even into my adult years, I was always so amazed and even envious of others who were masters of the left brain. They seemed to have it all. The world was their oyster, as they say. I watched them easily fit into the program of learning, retaining, synthesizing, regurgitating, and perpetuating words that wrapped ideas and concepts into perfect little end products. We were all taught how to generate consumables or services that were highly valued within the program and in turn perpetuated our given existence. We learned how to do this from our teachers and other grown-ups who lived within the bandwidth too – the container of all that was normal and admissible. I was especially in awe of those who could carve out a sense of happiness and fulfillment within the bandwidth. Believe me, they were far more popular at parties than I. Alas, the world and all of its valued knowledge and relative data have remained tiring, and even foreign to me throughout my life. Conversely, I was not only boring to those who were oriented to the left-brained stuff of the world. I noticed that I was barely visible – living in the misty fringes of normal, like a feminine ghost in the machine. And that was okay – preferable, actually.

I could not retain or memorize data that was irrelevant or not of use to me, so reading comprehension didn't click for me like I noticed it did for others. As one might guess, being tested on hollow data was my repeated nightmare throughout my school years. For me, acquiring a knowledge base without the correlation of direct experience was like trying to make glitter stick to paper without the glue. I seemed to be wired very differently than my classmates were, or perhaps I was slower to conform. They refer to this now as a learning disability, which was quite challenging for me throughout the public-schooling years, but I believe it turned out to be a good thing in the end.

I learned to adapt to this educational strangeness. I applied a deeper set of skills and senses that were available to me without thought, and I also carried this into my future work environments. Long story short, when presented with a question or task with just words and concepts, I used my intuitive skills to access and deliver the "right" answer or approach from the given container of data. I could do it, but it was exhausting. Thankfully, there was music. I believe it saved me, or at least helped me to rest in something that was more welcoming, nurturing, and resonant to the soul.

> *And that is the greatest gift of all to you… the realization*
> *that the sound of Creator can play through you… and it*
> *IS you.*

> ~ GOLD-LIGHT INTELLIGENCE

I'd like to speak about a kind of quantum marker that I experienced in my preteen years. I suppose it was both an echo from my past and a sign of things to come. By this point, I'd already dialoged with gold and blue angelic beings in the sandbox. I'd had numerous visitations in my bedroom, and I was levitated above my bed while simultaneously receiving telepathic downloads. I'd been taken out through the window and shot into space numerous times for more understanding that seemed to be set in interdimensional round tables and so much more. I had adapted to having a very secret nightlife with Gold-Light Angels and later a variety of others. All I knew was that no one ever spoke of such things. I assumed that maybe some of us did this at night, but we didn't discuss it in our waking lives – like so many other feeling experiences we pretend aren't real.

There are ways to time travel or transport our consciousness beyond the narrow bandwidth of our conditioning here. To do so, we don't have to first address the existence of angels, ETs on other planets, spaceships, or life in other solar systems, galaxies, and multiverses. They could be included in an imagined periphery, just as your family and friends are included in your lives here, but contact with a benevolent "more" is something that with your consciousness – including your physicality – you can choose to experience right now through your authentic feelings and voice. I discovered this, or popped into it, seemingly by accident early in my life. Then as an adult, I was given more detailed, yet still experiential, instruction on how to generate a resonant field to reconnect and realign with the rest of my Self. From this field, my Visitors were then accessible through the harmonics and overtones of my own signature frequency.

At around age eleven, I discovered an extraordinary passion for singing. It seemed to be built into my being. My parents were musical in their own ways, but I found little interest in their particular methods and styles. Back then, my mother's music revolved around church, and my father loved the old country tunes. My passion was born from a mysterious, almost reverent place within. The trouble was it seemed too far within because I couldn't find anything in my world that exactly matched what I longed to sound or create. Initially I couldn't sing my way out of a cardboard box. The conditioning in my life clearly informed me that I had no obvious ability to sing, but the fire within said differently. I was obsessed.

I sang in the family room for hours every day. After I got tired of singing along with early Elton John, Barbara Streisand, and Linda Ronstadt albums, I had a desire to produce the tones on my own. Singing a cappella was not enjoyable for me at the time, so it seemed appropriate to learn an instrument. My grandmother's old upright piano was donated to me, and after a few quick lessons from my mom about reading music and the correlation from dots on a page to the black and white piano keys, I was off on this learning side road. I was not passionate about playing the piano, and I'm still not to this day. However, it was necessary to support my next steps in the evolution of vocalizing.

Soon I was able to build a simple bed of piano chords so that I could read and sing these popular songs all by myself. It was delicious, this breakthrough. I loved it. My piano playing was terrible, but I didn't care. I had launched into singing out loud with my solo voice! Meanwhile, I was now in junior high school and simultaneously trying to fit in with both the program and my peers. These were exceedingly tough times. After the daily upside-down time at school and related social events, the many hours left in the day to lose myself in song was vital and provided a necessary healing. My life has always been an act of bouncing back and forth between the mundane and the unexplained. One moment I'm facing the school bully who has decided for the fourteenth time that I'm weird, and a good beating was in order; the next moment, I'm sitting on a piano bench, experiencing a surprise landing into the quantum power of resonance.

I had a small, shy singing voice at the time. It felt loud to me, but I soon became aware that I was holding back. How did I know? The Gold-Light Intelligence returned to be my vocal coach! No one was more surprised than I. Through a feeling-knowing instruction from within, I was directed to try this exercise, then another exercise following mastery of the first, and so on. These unconventional vocal-and-breathing aerobics went on until I had a significant, cardboard-box breakthrough. One afternoon I noticed that I was singing very loudly and with a force that I had not known was possible when I first ventured onto this path. It turns out that I needed this force later on – this wider opening to deliver sound. It helped me to land into ecstasy, no-time, and Pure Loving Presence.

I'm not completely sure, but I think I was singing Barbra Streisand's, 1977 hit, "My Heart Belongs to Me" [10] when it first happened. I reached one of the higher and more sustained notes, and I disappeared. Well, that is to say that the "I" that I perceived myself to be literally vanished from the reality that I had thought I was living in. It felt like I popped into an entirely new, huge-feeling reality. It was too beautiful to describe, and the power shook and reverberated deeply within the center of my being. Imagine diving deep within the nucleus of your being, and then continuing to dig down to synchronize with the heart of the Earth. At the same time, this power radiated out of my head, heart, and hands into infinity, where I became ultra-aware that I wasn't alone. In fact, I was completely at one with All.

The aspect of me that dug deeply within and the aspect that popped out into infinity circled back and fused together into a pure state of spherical, resonant awareness. I was no longer sitting on a piano bench in the family room singing a song from the pages of my music book. Instead, I was fused into the sound waves that I had been previously generating with my voice. I had no thought available to me, yet I was conscious of everything at once. I had landed into a network of absolute awareness.

Try explaining that one to your religious mother! Alas, my pure joy and excitement sped ahead – light years ahead – of any available 3D, teenage-girl vocabulary. As a result, I made no sense. I was left abandoned and naked in a language prison with little hope for translation to convey this divine "felt experience" to another human being.

In my mom's defense, I'm sure that I sounded certifiably insane – her daughter emerging from the family room in tears and rattling off excited, incoherent phrases. Indeed, in my expansive state, I had lost touch with the rules, boundaries, and social mores of the current reality. Upon my return to what others refer to as ordinary, I was re-triggered to the physical and emotional trauma of being judged and excluded from the normal club once again. All this occurred without my mother saying one word. Her fears had discharged into the air like toxic worry waves and continued to linger in the room even after she abruptly exited to pray for my healing. Little did she know that her "God [who] is Love" (a favorite Christian Science quote) was still quite present in our family room and beyond – through pure sound and resonance.

I believe the root of what she and others conditioned by religion are taught to be fearful of, subsequently call out as evil, and begin feverishly praying for in the wake of these unexplained happenings is for that damned too-many-feelings genie to be shoved back into the bottle. That which seems to be unexplained – outside known or church-ordained framing – must be quickly and securely stuffed back into the familiar box of our feelings-are-scary programming. In the end, it seems that actual feelings may be far too much for the smaller bandwidth of consciousness to process. Thus in the context of religion, talking, pontificating, and building identities and stories around our God *out there*, feels far safer than directly feeling and wholly resonating with IT *right here*.

There were more visitations, tonal happenings, and downloaded teachings from the Presence throughout high school. This continued to feed a growing cognitive dissonance and anxiety within me. It made me feel even more socially awkward and withdrawn from the normal behavior and activities of my teenaged peers.

Some of my clearest contact memories during this time had to do with waking up in the night and realizing that I was floating about four feet above my bed. The light forms stood at the foot and side of me as my bed was pushed up against a corner of my room. Sometimes they would fill the whole room – max capacity – as if this were *the* interdimensional hotspot to be. One notable perception on my part was that *another me* stood with them, and I was perfectly aware and on board with the purpose of these visits. When I, the human girl, would wake up into the realization that I was hovering above my bed, surrounded by a room full of nonhuman light forms, it was as if my local awareness was the last one to arrive to a party that had been going on for hours. At this point, the downloading into my heart-brain-body would initiate what I needed to know for the present time as well as into my future.

As desperately as I had wanted to share what was happening to me and, more importantly, what I was learning (or remembering), I discovered that it was quite hazardous for me to enter the explain-drain mode in my numerous attempts to describe these orientations with parents and friends. It disempowered me and zapped my life force energy, leaving me susceptible to low self-esteem, illness, and depression. In other words, when I adapted too far into the smaller mental spectrum in order to appear and communicate normally, I would compromise my own health and energetic balance. Additionally, I recall developing a ridiculous, over-the-top terror with speech. Communicating in empty words and memorized concepts was foreign and extremely difficult for me. I don't recall feeling truly at home with speech until I discovered and began practicing my own authentic voice. However, this didn't occur until far into the future.

What I understand more today is that if you and I were able to sound or resonate together in this vibrational place, neither one of us would need language or detailed explanations. Little did I know that this would be the entire theme of my life – having an actual felt experience, and then obsessively trying to find a resonant match for it in the world. Be they analogies, metaphors, or simply words in a book that I could point to, I was desperate to find the right language to share with others. Ultimately, my lifelong quest was born. I felt that people needed to know that this huge love is what ALL of human consciousness is connected to – a lost or missing piece that is longed for unconsciously that when suppressed or denied can perpetuate endless conflict, addictions, and countless misunderstandings.

Ah, but no one – and I mean no one – was interested in what I was passionately and privately engaged in. This lack of mirroring or validation in the upside-down world made me crazy. Soon I felt ashamed of being this strange young girl that people were either afraid of or made fun of or both. I literally had no one to inform me that I had value, and there was no outer appreciation for me – for just being me. I clearly see how this leads to an escalation of inauthentic masking or ways of being in order to survive and feel loved in the world.

During this time, my mother became more isolated. Still, she continued to quietly drive me from Barstow to Los Angeles for music rehearsals – two six-hour roundtrips a week. She spoke very little, but she knew it was important to me. At age fifteen, I had auditioned and was accepted into the musical singing group the Young Americans. I had found the announcement for tryouts in the choir room trashcan, the deadline less than a week away. When I asked why he didn't inform us, the teacher replied that no one in the Barstow High School Choir was qualified.

My mother continued to support my singing when she could, but eventually she sunk further into depression. I believe it was her way of coping with the growing contrast between her religion and my father's work, social life, and identity beyond home. He had an obvious longing for something more. They divorced before I turned sixteen. My father moved on – alive and excited again. He was building a life with his new love and her two young children. I had two older brothers who were busy finding and developing their own coping mechanisms from the pain and confusion of this unexpected derailment. The four of us – Mom, my brothers, and I – lived under the same roof for a time. There was love, but we rarely communicated beyond the superficial. It was further training for our lives to come – pretending everything was normal.

From that point forward, I seemed to be falling further into the abyss – where lost and confused human identities go. I had a unique knowing that I was completely loved for who I was by the visiting light forms that informed me so, but they never joined me for tea and scones at the corner cafe. This Presence was not interested in helping me to escape the excruciating hell that lies in the chasm between the finite and the infinite. They were there to inspire and encourage me to build a bridge. But for the time being, I had slipped and fallen in.

My extreme shyness and low self-esteem became so debilitating that I easily fell into agreement and resonance with those who scoffed and made fun of me. I now hated and judged myself for not being normal. By age seventeen, I had given up – shutting out most of who I was in order to conform and become more like other people. Being only a ghost-like shell of a human, I became ripe for possession by other humans who thrived in ignorance and psychopathy. As a result of temporarily losing my feeling connection to Source, I began to resonate with the self-hatred that magnetically attracted abuse at the hands of other lost and wounded human beings. This came in the form of sexual abuse, several attempted rapes, and relationships that perfectly mirrored the disdain and worthlessness I held for myself.

III

Re-Tuning to Self
Wait, Who Am I Again?

—∞∞—

We are called to be architects of the future, not its victims.

~ R. BUCKMINSTER FULLER

I felt that I was pretty much on my own after my parents' divorce. I suppose that's why I left home at a young age. For the next ten years, I would completely lose myself and any sense of personal direction. It was easy to submit to others' worldviews – especially when they seemed extremely confident in what they knew to be the truth, inconsistencies and all.

While I don't condone abuse of any kind, I do take full responsibility for unconsciously playing out the role of victim during this time. I was broken, and had lots of missing pieces. I was at a complete loss as to how to live and be on planet Earth. I desperately wanted someone to quickly fill in all the blanks. However, when you hand over that much power to other broken people and systems, it turns out they'll gladly take it. In other words, if you don't know thy Self, others will be happy to define you.

I was nineteen when I gave birth to my son. Most said that I was too young, but I knew it was the right thing to do. This time I did not succumb to the pressure to end the pregnancy, as I had done for the first. My son's birth, and his presence, is still the most glorious blessing of my entire life. In contrast, my relationship with his father was very difficult, to say the least. From the late 1980s to the early 1990s, I was in my mid- to late twenties. I was living in San Diego, and emerging from a string of deeply challenging events.

My mother passed away in the summer of 1985, following a slow, Christian Science, no-doctor–no-medicine death. It was just as her mother had passed several years earlier – the family matriarch of the religion. I learned how devastating it could be to allow someone you love to make the choice to slowly and painfully leave the body. A year or so before she got sick, she had remarried. He was a man who later proved himself to be incapable of genuine love. He didn't share her religion; however, he didn't seem unhappy with her choice to move on. While their marriage was short, he managed to have her sign an over-photocopied, one-page will that left him everything. I'm sure she had no idea what it was. We were unaware that she'd left her entire estate to him, which included generations of family treasures, real estate, and her bank account.

My brothers and I were completely powerless during her illness. The law protected her right to heal or die by the words of her religion's founder, Mary Baker Eddy. As she withered away in her bed, I couldn't stop crying and begging, "Please see a doctor, for us kids. *Please!*" Before she was transported to a designated Christian Science home for miraculous healings (or hushed-up endings), her parting words to me were, "Eileen. Oh, ye of little faith, I'm not going to die."

But she did.

It wasn't long after her death that the feeling to sing began leaking through my heart and back into my bloodstream again. This time, it wasn't just a passing phase. I could no longer suppress the need to recall who I was, find my voice, and sing it out into my world again. I get why a lot of people are afraid of change. I soon learned that even meekly calling out the need for change from within my highly controlled domestic environment caused an over-the-top, terrifying reaction.

I had chosen someone else's version of reality so that I could experience consistency. At the time, it probably never was consistent or anywhere near healthy for me, but the power of death has a way of breaking the spells of those left behind in its transformational wake. This had been my mother's parting gift, "Are you being yourself? Are you truly alive?"

It comes out of nowhere – the profound and soul-driven need to heal and find ourselves again. At the same time, it can't help but trigger and challenge everyone in our vicinity to either adapt to the transformation or try to stop it at all cost. On the other hand, it can feel paralyzing, intimidating, and even shaming to those who choose self-love and self-truth. I've learned that it's where we need to begin if evolution for the individual and the collective is desired. When the Soul speaks, we need to listen and gather courage, even in the face of violence and intimidation.

Sadly, the support, protection, and trauma therapies of the twenty-first century were not available to me in the 1980s. I suppose it didn't matter. At the time, I was completely unaware that I was deeply wounded and that I had made major life decisions from this damaged place. I assumed, as most people do, that this was life. Fortunately, my angel friends returned to inform me otherwise.

It was around 1986 that I found myself absolutely consumed by the need to sing again, and it could not be subdued. My vision and dream activity increased, and it seemed that every night I had visitors who shared – in their unique ways – the extreme importance that I wake up, move, sing, and locate my signature life force energy again.

The more I responded to this spirit of encouragement, the stronger I became. The harmonics generated from the initial states of reclaiming myself seemed to initiate an important intersection and magnetic attraction with others like me. It made sense. How could I find others like me if I wasn't actually being me?

I was still reeling over this challenge even as I sat with a small group observing a calm, studious-looking young man named Darryl Anka. Apparently, he was shifting his consciousness to meet the frequencies of an extraterrestrial named Bashar. I wasn't clear at all why I had felt so compelled to be there. Perhaps I should mention that my first experience of sitting with a medium or channeler was two years before this one, and it was nothing short of ridiculous. It was easily rejected. So what, pray tell, had I gotten myself into now? Within a few seconds of feeling the magnetic energy permeating the room and my body, it was very clear what I'd gotten myself into – frequency.

Before a word was spoken, I somehow knew all that I needed to know. It was as if I were instantaneously transported to my childhood again. My entire being was directly informed through this familiar, encoded field. I knew that I was completely at home with these energies and that I would now launch into greater vistas of understanding about my life in general, as well as personally own my growing sense of a dual identity.

Of course the years of discourse with words and humor were supremely enjoyable with Bashar as well. This Intelligence made me laugh as well as stretch – to see, remember, and trust what I already knew to be true about the nature of reality. However, it was quite clear that what I really needed and responded to naturally was in the calming, nurturing waves of resonance that I sank deeply into – occasionally playing with the ideas and words that danced on the surface.

Dialoging with both Darryl and his expanded Bashar-self provided my first mirror and validation for my own journey with ET visitors and guides. My unmet self, who had been drowning in swells of non-belonging anxiety, finally met a reflection *out there* that directly calmed my soul and matched my resonant truth within. As a result, the nighttime visits entered a completely new level of downloaded messages. During a series of lucid dreams in 1987, I was frequently fed tape after tape of what felt like endless data that was loaded directly into my head. This went on for several nights. The memory I had upon awakening from one of these events was what I recorded here in my journal:

Journal Entry: March 16, 1987
Bashar's presence was giving me a detailed, comprehensive description of the way the world and people would transform

over the next several decades. He included dates or times that went well into the 2000s. He also talked about how Darryl would change and how I would change too. We were alike and would similarly transform and bridge our higher or future selves into one being. I'm not remembering specific words or details because it seemed to have been all through higher-sensory feeling that it was transmitted to me... higher-realm conversation.

When I awoke, I knew how important the dream was, so I tried to recall what was specifically conveyed. I could not, but then I knew that I had absorbed it anyway, and it didn't matter that I couldn't verbalize it.

Darryl and I have stayed in touch over the years. Recently I reminded him of these 1987 dream conversations. Together we explored the message about bridging from our *now* vantage point, "well into the 2000s." He is releasing a documentary about his life and work at the time of this writing. I'm proud of and thrilled for him, and I also see what an incredibly important story he has to tell. I know how vital and empowering it is to my well-being – witnessing the hidden and taboo aspects of my Self, finally being displayed outside and *out loud* on the collective world screen. It was exactly what I needed – the sweet validation from mirrors – other humans living truthful, courageous, yet highly unconventional lives.

From my vantage point, I clearly see that these heart-resonant influences and experiences, along with many more to come, were key in supporting my integration and overall well-being. It was so that I could continue to grow, expand, and stay the course.

Singing in solitude had always been necessary for me to stay aligned with guidance and the feeling reminders of my authentic Self. As was usual, though, I was unable to stay comfortably alone with this private joy for long. I was being prodded from within to overcome my ridiculous fear of singing in front of an audience.

After finding other musicians to perform with, via the local *San Diego Reader Magazine* (the Craigslist of the time), we worked quickly to establish and rehearse a repertoire of favorite oldies and popular dance songs. It took months of surviving anxiety attacks and many tearful declarations that, "It was all so hopeless," and "I give up," before I finally faced and broke through my extreme fears of singing in public. After this milestone, it began to go very, very well but not without consequences.

These so-called selfish desires on my part upset the established, unconscious agreement that I stay small and self-loathing within my personal relationship. I had dared to express my true nature. It wasn't long before it clearly became unhealthy and unsafe for me to stay.

"Move," as Bashar stated to me during a Los Angeles group event, "On all levels, *move*. Move before the circumstances of what you have created prevents any movement at all." This source of soul guidance had proven itself to be highly valuable many times over. He had said it with such love and such force that I knew it was imperative to act.

As the walls were closing in on me, I prayed to God, to the angels, and even to the sea, "Please let us get out of this alive and whole. I promise if I live through it, I'm all yours, forevermore."

I left.

After five months of feeling non-stop anxiety, terror, and uncertainty, I found a foothold and began to feel the ground again. Also, for the first time in my young adult life, I was able to explore what existed beyond the oppression and abuse that I had unconsciously agreed to in the teen and early-adult years of my life.

"Forgive," it said.

Of course I resisted the inner suggestion to forgive. *Are you effing kidding me?* Yet this was when I learned how powerful the act of forgiveness could be. It dispelled all the fearful assumptions that if I forgave, my perpetrators would get away with what they had done to me. Wrong. It is not my responsibility to manage others' choices. I was shown that when we take the initiative to forgive, this Presence will reinforce the truth of who we are so that we can make more conscious life choices through self-love and self-valuing – from that moment forward. As a result, I transcended the pain, fear, and self-loathing that I had once agreed to cage myself in, and the bars dissolved – at least enough for me to continue the climb toward my own sense of self again.

Forgiveness is about our own healing. It isn't connected whatsoever to what abusers choose to be or do for the rest of their lives. These things are best given over to the sea.

Meanwhile, my outer world of growth and expansion into the music scene was reflecting back to me that I and my voice had value, so I set myself on a track to use my voice in the ways that paid. This meant singing in nightclubs and at private parties – from the large corporate type to small weddings and ceremonies. There were many periods that I enjoyed a work schedule of performing five to six times a week. Still, as a single mom not receiving any additional monetary support, it became painfully clear that I required more income to provide for my son and me. This was the beginning of an awkward, lifetime dance between what I loved to do and what I needed to do to survive in the world.

As strange as it sounds, I was always quite good at admin-organizational and numbers work, so getting hired was pretty easy at the time. However, staying with it, due to the rapid loss of soul and imagination, was extremely challenging. I progressed through a few high-tech company transfers and promotions and ultimately ended up in the employ of one of the largest defense contractors in the world. With my secret clearance, I found myself involved in special classified projects that happened in special ironclad rooms. Ironically, while the walls were getting thicker around me, the visits and contact grew in full force.

This was my random-daytime-ecstatic-states period of contact, as well as numerous nighttime surgeries and resonant pep talks. Before this time, all of my visits had occurred in the comfort of home or other safe locations that were out of the public eye. Understand that many of these visits, each time they occurred, had a way of wiping clean the whole hard drive of my established worldview and way of life. To this day, I have no idea how I managed to climb out of bed after these mind-blowing nights and get myself to work. I just knew I had to – all of this without anyone in my work or private life truly knowing what I was experiencing.

Lucid dream Experience: May 5, 1987

After just a few moments of lying still in bed after retiring for the night, I heard and felt a voice. It felt clear, and I was quite at ease with it. It said we were going to accelerate the process. Truths were then recited about inner wisdom, and I also experienced a seamless, back-and-forth dialog with it. I fell asleep. I awoke into an active, lucid-dreaming state. It felt like teachings had been on-going. Soon the stage changed, and I was channeling. My eyes were closed, but there were scribbles of communication occurring in my mind's eye. It indicated that I was translating and channeling to an audience. I saw and felt myself fully immersed in water with the high-frequency chatter and play of dolphins surrounding me. I would then emerge from this state and open my eyes. There were so many people taking notes, smiling, and tearfully happy, and then they were begging me to go back and do it again. I was moving in and out of this "linking" state. When I would open my eyes again, I was hoping that the audience would tell me what was happening, but they were just so eager for me to continue, to go within and do it again.

Note: Later I would share this experience at a large Bashar event in Los Angeles in June 1987 – the Convergence Session. I was terrified to approach the mic and ask about this experience and…was I a channel? Bashar had fun with me – as if to say, this is funny that you behave as if you don't know. He added that there was no great, lengthy process for me to go through. I could begin whenever I was ready.

Visitation: Early May 4, 1990

I had alien contact again. Before I opened my eyes, I was aware that I was lying down while they were above and surrounding me. There were many hands touching me. I was naked on a soft table in what felt like an operating room. I'll never forget what I felt. Their hands and fingers were very long and slender, and their skin felt like warm, soft rubber. I remember feeling like, "Oh, just another routine healing," but then I had a growing awareness of their high-pitched energy as they worked mostly around my abdomen. It rapidly shifted into a fever-pitch current of sexual intensity. I recall that I made no connection between what they were doing and my independent need to stop or "resolve" my situation. They must have picked up the cues of my increasing discomfort and caught my hand as it jerked from my side involuntarily. They very gently returned my hand to my side and telepathically communicated that they understood my body's reactions, but it was very important that I know it wasn't about human sexuality at all. It was how my current vibration interpreted the higher frequency through the distortions of my conditioning. I was further told that one day I would integrate and understand this phenomenon completely. [Note: Sometimes during telepathy, it's like I can feel their need to emphasize something (mid-sentence) by energetically pressing further into my head. It's happened enough that I thought I should write it here.]

Visitation: May 30, 1990

I woke up from my dream – into that fever-pitch lucid state. I know this very well now. My knees were on my pillow at the head of my bed as I leaned onto the ledge of my open window. There was no screen. I felt the perfectly cool air cascade across my skin. I gazed up at a huge disk-shaped spacecraft as it slowly departed. There was a sweet smile on my face. I felt so much joy. It can't fit into words. Lingering in the room was their energy – such deep love and appreciation.

I was well aware of the inherent blessings from each interaction, yet I told only a few close friends back then and in the most cursory of ways. Even a hip local minister became tongue-tied when I asked whether he'd heard of such things. I quickly learned that there was no way to explain these rapid shifts in consciousness without the listener's fears being triggered. Thankfully, I'd had more experience and enough breakthroughs to process my own fear about the high-vibratory nature of these visits. I was good with it for the most part, but having other humans to join me in this between-worlds space would've been incredibly comforting. In the end, even the young, cool minister said it was probably the tricks of Satan. Not cool at all.

Visitation-Dream Conversation: February 22, 1991

I became aware of or woke up midstream in a dream conversation. I was being informed about my future job (if I chose) to become a mediator of sorts between nonhuman intelligence and humans, to assist in communication between the two. They pointed to my natal horoscope chart with Uranus opposition Mercury from the ninth to third houses, which indicates a prior-birth commitment. (I'm remembering and writing this at work and imagining some-one finding and reading this. Oh, Dear God!)

The following journal account is one that I used later as a foundation for a solo performance. In 2012 I had rewritten it to be lighter and more en-tertaining and humorous for an audience. I never performed it, so it feels better to return it to its more authentic, raw form:

Visitation: May 24, 1991, San Diego, CA

I knew it was going to happen again on this particular night. It was the growing background noise in my head, a very pleasant tickling around my fingers and lips, and a warming in my heart, neck, and scalp. It was so pleasant that it quite successfully wiped out any thought of anxiety about another rendezvous with the unknown. It was curious that they'd decided to have a meet up on this night – when my eleven-year old son was staying over at his father's house. In the past, it didn't seem to matter to my Visitors whether my son was in the next room or not. Still, I enjoyed the sweetness of the vibrational announcements as I washed the dishes, turned off the TV, and prepared for bed. I had no indication that this night would be any different, except for a strange, butterflies-in-the-belly feeling that the experience was going to be bigger than usual.

Following the last few visits from my cosmic friends, while my son was sound asleep in his room, I would awaken to all the lights turned on in the condo. There was also the loud click-clack, click-clack of my out-of-control answering-machine next to the bed. It seemed to be an eerie, off-rhythm sort of percussion track laid under and mixed into the musical sounds of my loudly blasting stereo. It was always some random, popular 90's song broadcast from a local San Diego FM station. It would fill the night air from my living room speakers, out into the parking lot, and beyond. I could never figure out how it happened, but when it did, I would systematically fly out of bed and dive first for the volume knob. Then I would more slowly and robotically turn off the lights and other small electronics that had also turned on. It was as if they too couldn't help but join in on the electromagnetic symphony of light and sound. The last stop would be a peek through my son's door to see whether the interruption in silence and normalcy had disturbed him. I was always so relieved when it had not. As strange as it sounds, I was used to it. Soon I'd be back in my bed, rubbing my arms to calm the hairs that stood on end. My thoughts would eventually slow down, and off I would drift into the nothingness.

On this night, I was in the nothingness again – lost in a deep, comfortable, and much-needed sleep. I was a long way off from a thought or worry of any kind. Then it all changed.

It was as if a massive shockwave slammed into me, and the sound of my own gasps and vibrating panic convulsed me awake. My whole body felt as if it had been punched, yet there was no outer evidence that anyone was there. No one actually physically hit me, but I can tell by my inability to breathe and the evidence of my pounding heart that soon my life would be over or never be the same again. The feeling of impending death was creeping and expanding into the air, like a thick fog all around me. I wasn't able to think normally, but I recall the feeling that someone was here to kill me. I couldn't open my eyes, but they were there, on the opposite wall across from my bed, watching me. I was paralyzed and completely out of my mind with fear. I wanted death to come quickly. I knew I couldn't sustain this level of fear in my heart and body and survive anyway. Please, I thought, just kill me.

Before I knew it, I was instantly pulled to a sitting position by the rush of an unseen force. The panic increased to a level beyond what I felt was possible. Mind you, this is coming from someone who has danced with otherworldly beings, in her bedroom no less, too many times to count. Something had changed.

I find now that I am far beyond any control of my mind, my body, and my feelings. Someone or something is in my bedroom with a clear intent to meet with me, but I see and know nothing except that I am drowning in terror. Just when I think I will pass out and die, I feel long, thin fingers slowly and firmly grip both of my ankles at the same time. These persistent, otherworldly hands are then slowly pulling me down to the foot of the bed until I reach the very edge and slip off. My butt hits the floor, but not in a painful way that one would expect with the given height and gravity. I am now completely helpless, yet I am still able to perceive or hear that I'm crying. One strange thing that I remembered at this point was that when I ran out of breath from one long string of sobs, I was aware that I put a distinct question mark lift in tone at the end – as if to ask, "Why?" in the only way that I could. Would my murderers grant me the decency of a response?

I am unable to move from this position – frozen, propped up with my back against the bed. I then have a thought, a brilliant solution from my conditioned brain. The Lord's Prayer will protect me from whatever this is. Even though the last time I remember reciting it was when I was twelve – in defiant protest and sitting on a pew at my mother's Christian Science Church. Over and over I regurgitate the words as if they were the best line of defense for that which has no defining word or context. "Our Father, which art in Heaven, hallowed be thy name..." The words turned into gibberish. The terror prevented my mouth, or anything for that matter, from functioning. I stopped trying to talk and sobbed quietly.

The sheer insanity of my state is soon interrupted by a question. It's coming from them, but I still can't see anything, and I can't actually physically hear any words being spoken. The question is echoing within my brain,

"Do you know that you have a choice? What you are experiencing now with this interaction is a choice of fear. The other choice is love. Would you like to change your experience to one of love?"

I can't respond. Part of me is still madly trying to figure out what this is and how I am even hearing these words in my head with no sound. Again they offer, "Do you choose this interaction with fear or love?" Then the energy, or force of it, pressed into my head even further, "What is your answer?"

"LOVE!" I blurted out, surprising myself with the sound of my own voice, as it seemed to be coming from across the other side of the room. It was odd, but at this point, I couldn't think or process anything beyond just noticing it. This was a pivotal moment in my experience, this night as well as my whole life. They heard me. And Love changed everything. Terror transformed into indescribable peace and beauty. It filled me from my heart within, throughout my body, and throughout the whole room. What felt like an enemy before – out to kill me – was now a huge presence with wisdom and compassion that radiated beyond the known world. Yet the love was too large for my little mind, my little heart, and my little body. I just knew there had to be someone or something in charge of modulating the frequency. There had to be. Otherwise, I would blow up into a trillion little pieces – like a glass shattering from the powerful waves of a cosmic opera.

This massive current of love differentiated into a light being, or two. They were tender and caring. I was slowly and gently lifted off the floor, and they began moving me. Rather, I'm floating with increasing speed toward my bedroom window. A thought rings out, like my voice did earlier from across the room, "Shouldn't we open the window?" Before I knew it, the noise in my head was growing louder and louder. Then I'm aware that I'm passing directly through the glass. I felt myself as a collection of extremely relaxed molecules, like stars with an infinity of dark matter in between. It's like I knew how to work with the atomic level like this, to move through solid objects. Once I passed all the way through the window and re-collected myself, I was aware that I was actually hovering about twenty feet above my car in the condo parking lot – but not for long.

Bam! I am blasting away in what feels like supersonic and very loud speed to a distant point in space, where I stop as suddenly as I had started. And I'm floating again. I'm in the buoyant, watery mix of an infinite number of brilliant stars and galaxies. I enjoyed it for a time before an orchestrator of sorts stepped in to hit the download button on his console. I was quite familiar with this part of it. It's happened many times before. Massive amounts of data are pouring into an expanding storage database within my cells. The same data that was filling me up within was being mirrored onto the starry, 360-degree cosmic screen around me. A variety of geometrical figures are gently drifting by in just the right timing – like the most epic PowerPoint presentation one can imagine. The detail was incredible. I recall seeing giant 3D views of pyramids, tetrahedrons, octahedrons, and other varieties of geometrical figures that I'd never, ever seen before. All of them would slowly spin and light up in certain areas to emphasize what was being delivered. Then our human DNA floats by and stops. There was a special focus on this part of the presentation.

The DNA was huge in its presence above me, and it seemed that someone pressed the slow-rotation button so that I could really take this one in. The entire experience lasted for what seemed like days or weeks, and in a strange sort of nonsensical way, it even felt as if it could be another whole lifetime.

I know this presence. It's so familiar, yet this appointment in time was significantly more intense – like a scheduled reminder for me to wake up from the dream as well as nudge me into a mandatory leap in consciousness. As shocking and uncomfortable as this all had begun, before I changed my perspective, I realized that the life that I'd been living back there in the San Diego condo was fast becoming more like the dream. And what I was experiencing here – floating in space with the stars and my familiar friends – is more like the real world. This degree of real is etched into every molecule of my body – forevermore.

Bam! I literally slam back into my body in my bed in the condo in San Diego. My eyes open wide with a quick intake of air, and I release it with a hearty laugh. Really? Seriously? A Pointer Sisters' song is blasting out through the condo and into the night air.

"I'm So Excited, and I just can't hide it. I'm about to lose control, and I think I like it." Intelligent with a sense of humor – it was as if they needed to add a certain punctuation to the overall experience. This is about expansion, yes, but with joy and excitement. No more fear.

I robotically followed through with my usual after-contact routine. I turned off the radio, the lights, my answering machine, and any analytical thought. I needed to get some sleep. Like always, tomorrow was another day, and I had to go to work.

After each extreme interruption in my desperate attempts for a normal life, I alone would step through the slow and methodical process of adapting to and integrating a larger bandwidth of consciousness – over months and sometimes years. Incidentally, it was a few years later that I was introduced to the book, *A Course in Miracles*. Imagine my surprise and joy when reading and then recalling the same life-changing message from my Visitors: "In every new moment, we always have a choice as to how to experience it – with love or fear." Following May 1991, I never experienced fear to this degree with contact again or anything, really. I understood completely that it was always my choice.

The "I" that is writing this book today has integrated the visits of the past – purely through feeling and knowing and the passing of time. Clearly, there was no mental infrastructure in place for assimilating the events into everyday life, and there was no outer explanation as to why it was happening to me. Still, I was being pressed to blow up my own psyche's conditioned infrastructure and worldview – repeatedly. It forced me to rebuild from a new foundation, every time, but beyond that, I had no further details that made sense.

I was determined to keep my sanity – if not for me, then for the well-being of my son. Actually, it was being a mother of this amazing human being that would later become the last-stop, conscious thought before arresting my own attempts at suicide.

IV

Breaching the Boundaries
Annihilating Normal

———⟨∞⟩———

"Abductees," Eva said, "are souls that have, for their
individual purposes and reasons, chosen the
probability of physical form. But through their experiences
they are regaining their memory of source...
The process of abduction is one form of such,
of regaining memory. The abduction experience itself,"
Eva said, "is a mechanism to remove the structures
that impede the reconnection with source and to
purify the physical vehicle in such a way to
serve to regain better memory and to
bring knowledge to others." [11]

~ EVA, ABDUCTEE

During the early 1990s, after years of wiped-out world views and reintegration segments, my Visitors seemed to develop a curiosity about my job and workplace. I found myself typing and compiling classified technical documents as the familiar Love energy blended and filled my body. While my supervisor trusted that I was rapidly typing top secret equations and text, many times I was helplessly ensconced in full ecstatic states with tears running down my face. This, along with the lovely hand dancing, and foreign-sounding words pouring out of my mouth. The energies would fuse into me as if to demonstrate what making love was truly supposed to feel like.

From that point on, while enjoyable, I found that human sexuality registered only a tiny blip on the universal screen of what was possible. These ecstatic states were top secret all right. If these things were going to happen beyond my own bedroom, it very well should be contained within a classified vault.

Concurrently, I was keeping up with a part-time musical career, and by the early to mid-1990s, I was collaborating and performing with San Diego-based original music bands. The distance between everyday consciousness and hyperaware states of union was causing a great divide within my consciousness again. I was perpetually torn between using all my energy to fit into the status quo or honoring the transforming self that routinely wandered beyond the boundaries of known consciousness. I was aware that in one direction I would have to trust in the smallness of the conditioned world. In the other direction, I was being asked to trust the pure feelings generated by these loving light beings – the ones who directly contacted my heart. If one has no direct experience and no high-contrasting reality in which to reconcile, I suppose it would be quite easy to dismiss all of this. During these times, I found myself begging again for normal, but it never came.

I remarried in the mid-1990s – to my best friend. It didn't last as long as I'd hoped, though. In response to my dire need to be normal inside and out, I married a gentleman whose picture was in the dictionary next to the word "normal." I loved him, and I was convinced that our marriage would serve as the bridge between the extremes in my life. I thought that I could literally marry normal and the unknown would stop knocking at my door. We bought the cookie-cutter house with the picket fence and pink rosebushes, but my mission to normalize failed when the visits came back in very surprising ways.

Journal Entry: March 19, 1995

I awoke from a dream with a yell and sat up in my bed. The alien vibration had created such a powerful orgasmic feeling in my whole body that I had to make sounds. The energy stayed with me as I lay awake for about twenty minutes. It was about 3 a.m. I was able to communicate thoughts and receive telepathic impressions back about what was going on. I was told it was a blending reaching to the physical level. I almost felt like I was someone else, or there was something angelic within me, but it was still me. (I know this sounds strange.) My body and face moved in ways I was not consciously activating. I wanted to make huge sounds as well, but curbed that as much as possible as to avoid waking D (my husband). At one point, I wanted to tell D what was going on, but in the next moment, I knew that I shouldn't. I'm convinced that he's subdued during these interactions anyway. He must be, to sleep through the sounds and movements I make. The response was loving but said that I would understand more when I needed to.

Journal Entry: December 23, 1995

D was out Xmas shopping, and I had been reading. I felt a presence but as usual ignored it for a while. It persisted. I put the book down and recited the Lord's Prayer. I felt at peace almost immediately. It's a warm, melting feeling, like the drug Demerol felt after surgery years ago. It was only a moment before I felt a persona. A smile crossed my face, and then I heard the telepathic words, "We missed you. Welcome back." It was good to feel the power and peace again, as I had been trying to hold it at a distance. I couldn't deal with reconciling crazy now. I had been sick with a pain in my lower-left abdomen. An energetic focus started to build there. Encouraging, calming words echoed in my heart. I saw a white light as they narrated going through my small and large intestine. It was melting any obstructions or unhealthy tissue, and it left bright, white, radiant tissue behind. "All is well," it said. There was a shift. My energy seems to take a huge and sudden leap to a higher frequency. I then recognized myself as a chief or leader in the Maya culture. I got, "Prince of Peace" (isn't that a Jesus thing?) as I sensed this incredibly powerful, earthy energy. He spoke to me saying that he is a leader because of his connection to Earth. SHE always guides him in leading his people.

As this was going on, I was getting a clear visual – of me. I felt and looked very strong. I was very connected to the earth as I sat in a throne-like chair. It seemed that I wore a very tall, feathered hat/headdress and a necklace draped my neck and shoulders. I was bare except for a skirt-like material wrapped on my waist. He was teaching me, but it was me. His guidance was to follow his way in reconnecting with Earth. "Feel it!" – resounded within. Then I felt the strong, magnet pull from my feet to the earth and heard the message in my head, "Use her wisdom to be a leader and to guide your people. (I wondered whether he was talking about singing? My mind wanted to find a correlation as to why he spoke about me this way. Anyone that knows me would agree. I'm not the leader type.) He said, "You have this within you," and then very firmly added, "Use it!"

My head dropped and my eyes opened. When I started to have a "Yeah right, I'm insane" feeling, I stopped myself and remembered that I had made an earlier agreement to welcome these incidents without judgment. I recalled that my whole face had changed; it became chiseled, stern, and powerful. My lips had tightened, and my jaw was masculine feeling. I felt him as a truly spiritual man. He then manifested outside of me (in mind's eye) on the living room floor near the fireplace. He was so strong with his next message that I wondered whether I should be afraid. "No. Listen," was the response within. He then crouched down and pounded the floor as he said loudly and quite determinedly, "It's ALL ABOUT THE MOTHER NOW. It's time to do the work. MOVE! NOW!"

This above experience had proven to be one of my most crazy and most significant ones. The significant part wouldn't be clear until many years later. It was difficult, but I trusted.

Journal Entry: January 29, 1996

As I lay in bed, waiting for sleep to come, I felt a familiar energy and presence fill the room. I switched back to childhood, as it was the same no-time feelings. I was the little girl and the grown woman, feeling the anxiety build inside of me. I didn't want to fear it, but it just happens. I said a prayer of protection and I blacked out. I woke up within the lucid encounter state.

Light beings were outside on the street and floating back and forth through my window. I was being shown several pages of writing, and I was getting a ton of information again. Learning so much. The writing was beyond foreign to the human part of me, but I understood it quite clearly in the dream experience. It was a series of squiggly symbols, lines, and dots. There were other unexplained elements too – like there were other dimensions that lit up above the pages. It was normal for this language to be multidimensional.

The vibration was quite high because there was that constant, borderline anxiety. I woke up feeling wonderful and at peace.

Journal Entry: March 17, 1996

[Went to bed sick, abdominal cramping and general malaise. I've had slim-to-none in the way of periods, and the size of my belly has grown over the past several weeks. Pregnancy test is negative. The magnetic energy "pulled me" to go to bed at 7:30 p.m.]

Lucid dream: I remember giving birth to a baby girl. There were several other nondescript forms around me in the dark. I didn't completely understand what was going on until after laboring over something. I noticed that I was naked, and my legs were spread in stirrups of sorts. I reached down and felt a tiny foot sticking out of my vagina. Another wavelike contraction came over me with no pain, just the sheer, ecstatic pleasure of my body pulsing to bring the baby out. I tried to push but couldn't feel that it helped. She then slipped out easily and effortlessly. I looked her over, seeing her genitals first to identify her sex (more female than male looking). She was very, very small, looked odd, and cried through the birth matter on her.

I called out to the others standing around me and wondered whether she needed a doctor's care. They just stayed in the shadows and watched – seeming to be female, about five feet tall, and with veils over their faces. I gathered that all would be okay. I loved this little being so much, and I was so happy to be holding her. At first her not-quite-human appearance shocked me, but when our eyes met, it was as if All of Creation was alive and awake within her. This is when the dream became even more heightened. There was so much love and recognition between us.

One of the adult ET females stepped forward and spoke inside my head. She wasn't just going to take her without confirming our original agreement. I instantaneously understood that our agreement was that I surrender her to their care. Straight ahead was a large arched doorway. I knew that down the hall to the right was where they kept the babies. I felt so much love for these female midwives, and while I understood the importance of this plan, it was still quite painful to hand her over.

I'm crying now because I miss her and I feel an emptiness and a longing for her. [Note: I grieved for several months in my waking life. It was a difficult process to have so much grief but no outer representation of loss in my waking life.]

It continued a few months later:

Journal Entry: May 6, 1996
Lucid dream: I was holding my hybrid daughter. She began nursing from my right breast. The beings stood again in the

shadows – maybe four or five of them witnessing the event. I felt the strong heart sensations move from me through my breast to her. I cried out with the power that was moving through me. There was a sense or nod from the witnessing beings that they were honored to be present for this interdimensional, cocreated experience. So much love.

As I type these journal entries on the page, I can't help but have compassion for the Eileen that I was back then. She did not have the context that I do now. I'm not saying that I have a lot of context now, but when I tap back into this 1990s, still-trying-to-be-normal girl, I love her deeply, and I greatly admire her courage to trust this ever-present, guiding Love.

Journal Entry: July 29, 1996

They paid a visit last night. I'm crying now, with joy, as I still feel this perfect love that envelops me. It was about 1 a.m. D was still not to bed. I was in and out of consciousness, aware of the love bath and then losing consciousness into dreams and symbols. I woke up out of this, but I couldn't move, except my hands moved on their own over my heart, and I moaned from the vibrational ecstasy.

Between soundings, in one of the transitions of breath, I got a clear visual on a being. He was animate and real. The eyes were liquid at the widest part of the head. The face tapered quickly to a pointed chin. Somehow, he seemed so familiar, not the kind of "seen him in books" familiar.

A myriad of those symbols – squiggles, angles, and dots – began to form around the perimeter of his face and within his eyes. It was a whole different kind of language. It then faded. I woke up a little while later recalling everything. The energy was gone enough so that I could move on my own and go to the bathroom. I still retained that magnetic buzz even after climbing back into bed.

Journal Entry: November 17, 1996

My son woke me up around 9 a.m. Got home from the gig last night around 1 a.m. We ate breakfast, and I decided to go for a walk. I started to change my clothes but became overwhelmingly tired and crawled back into bed. I had a series of "can't move, no energy, exhausted" dreams.

Suddenly, I became lucidly aware of being on a table, face down. I can't tell whether I'm still in my room or in another operating room. In my mind's eye, I could see several beings around me discussing the procedures they would be performing on me. They started the procedure through my back and behind my heart. It felt like highly pressurized energy pouring in and then oozing into the realm of my head, neck, shoulders, and arms. They discussed something else about the next area and then went for it. It was painful. It felt like a scalpel incision across the width of my middle back.

At this point, I was very afraid and started to pray – no known phrases, just a focus on God and asking him to care for me. The female voice was strong behind my right ear, making a statement about timing in my life. She said something about after June 2 things would really get going – not her words, my paraphrase.

These beings were very strong and almost emotionless with a very specific job to do. I remembered later that they asked for my permission to proceed. It was put in a personal way, like, "Are you ready for the next phase?"

Journal Entry: December 3, 1996

Lucid dream: I found myself flying through many different people's lives. I was like electricity that could take on any form I wished. At one point, I remember changing into sound. I remember there was a low horn sound, and then I responded playfully with a high, "Honk-honk." I didn't make the sound. I was the sound.

I had such fun through the whole experience. There were no rules. I felt that the experience was to remind me to lighten up and remember the illusory nature of the things and situations in my life. It was difficult to pull myself out of this nap. In a half-awake state, I saw the same small woman I had seen about four years ago, floating in my bedroom. The one who said, "Make way for one who is sweeter." Her energy was so beyond any sweetness I'd ever felt. She has beautiful long, blonde hair, and she's about a foot tall. This time she was hovering toward the ceiling by the door wearing a stunning, aqua-colored gown. The color was indescribable, not like anything here. Who is she?

Journal Entry: March 27, 1997
Lucid dream: I went to hear a woman singer perform. I listened for a bit, and then she shared a song that had a phenomenal effect on me. It was a song to and from our Source. The lyrics, music, and voice were so beautiful that I cried. The expansive feelings were magnificent. I spoke with her later and expressed my joy and gratitude. She was so beautiful, with long, blond, wavy hair that flowed down to her ankles. She reminded me of the woman in the aqua gown. She came to one of my shows later. She said she enjoyed it, but she chose not to do that kind of music anymore – just the prayer songs now. In the dream, I felt the inspiration to write these kinds of songs – ones that deeply moved me.

Journal Entry: May 14, 1997
D and I are on the West Coast of Florida at one of his best friend's homes. Earlier in the day, we had a great time at the beach and ate some incredible food. The first day had worn me out, so I lay down in the guest room to take a nap. I felt the energy or presence that I haven't felt in a while. I had to moan quietly with the

surges of pleasurable energy. Before this, I was not feeling pleasure; I was exhausted and crabby.

After sleeping for a few hours, I awoke with surges of energy coursing through my body. Someone turned it up to high. I
couldn't make myself become fully conscious, but I did toss and
turn some. When I lay still on my back for a moment, my hands
went up and moved on their own. It's one of the most glorious
things I've ever felt, but I remember wanting it to stop because it
was too much for the time and place. Eventually it did, but it took
a while. I had mixed feelings. "I want this" and "It's too much to
deal with this on vacation in someone's guest room!"

Trust me, these activities (and many more) were not conducive to traditional marriages. As you might guess, our pink roses and picket fences
were eventually obliterated. My husband and I divorced four years later. He
remarried not long after our divorce and had two, beautiful children. His
new wife strongly advised him against ever contacting me again. Naturally,
this broke my heart, as he had been my best friend for years. Still, I'm truly
happy that he found the life and love that supported the most rewarding
(and normal) life for him.

By 1997, I was completely unable to continue with the band or the
day job. I had reached a breakdown of sorts. I knew that I could no longer
endure what seemed to be the next level of dualistic agony – between my
outer acceptable identities and the continued program with my visitors.
Everything shut down. I suppose these days it would be called severe depression, but I call it a life-or-death standoff with my soul. It was a deep
quaking within my core – a presence that was no longer willing to be
pushed to the sidelines or back to the basement of my consciousness. It
was time to reconcile with a soul that intimately knew its Source and was
demanding that the wayward, or localized, "I" on Earth join back up with
the team.

Simply stated, we had reached the end of the divided road, and I was being highly pressured from within to embrace and live my singular truth. As scary and desperately lonely as it was, my life and voice needed to be more honest, integrated, and authentic. This was an absolute prerequisite for the work ahead, but as usual, there was not a human in sight who could provide the road map.

V

The Lost and Found Years
Dangling between Death and Life

—⌘—

Take me to the battlefield
Where I can fight and fall and heal
At least until I find what's true, what's real
Take me from the only love I've known
So I will find this time
And I will find the road back home
Where I am loved
Where I am touched
With a grace that I can feel
With a heart that is healed
You are awakening me
To free[12]

~ E. Meyer (Lyrics)

At the close of the century, three years of an energetic healing school seemed to be a move in the right direction. Still, what I thought was going to happen after graduation was what most students assumed – that I was going to set up shop as a vibrational healer. I could have, and along with my lifetime of lessons in higher-frequency contact, the career choice made sense. However, once again the Gold-Light Intelligence showed me that, yes, my soul is all about healing and transformation, but the greater unfolding at the time was that it wouldn't be limited to a hands-on approach. Making music by utilizing my voice to translate inspiration into melodies and words would become the dominant energetic healing form.

In 1998, after quitting my life as I had known it – previously defined as a musical entertainer and administrative day jobber – all I did was rage and cry. I was alone now. My now-teenage son was spending more time away from home, having entered the world of music, friends, and eventually college. Day in and day out, my life was about expressing the deepest, darkest, abandoned parts of myself.

Directing my tantrums and ultimatums at the God as defined by my Christian Science mother, I persistently threatened to take my own life. What other option did I have? I had decided that as a freak of the unnatural world, I held absolutely no value, no purpose, and no reason to continue.

Even though I had to keep up an occasional positive face to friends and family in the outer world, mostly I kept myself secluded away from everyone. I have memory glimpses of being completely out of my mind – distraught with weeping on the kitchen floor, the bedroom floor, in the shower (when I had the available energy), and in my car. I would drive to the store, the mountains, and the beach to numbly sit and stare. But mostly, I drove myself into oblivion.

One day, not long after weeks of these epic fits of rage, I woke up and felt very different. I went to the kitchen to make coffee. There was a calm centeredness about me that was new and interesting. I sat down, took a few sips, and *felt* a question. It surprised me at first, as it was loudly heard, but it didn't originate outside of me. I did my best to respond, and while it had some energetic markers to my frequent visitors of the past, I wasn't completely sure who was asking and who was responding.

"Are you ready to proceed?"

"Yes," I said, matter-of-factly, but I was highly aware that my response was coming more from a core identity than the one who had been previously rampaging. Where did she go? It was a question born from mild interest but not as interesting as who was present now.

I tried again, slowly and methodically, "Yes? I feel pretty good. Uh, this is new."

Nothing more came. *Oh well. Sigh.* After a few minutes of sipping my coffee and wondering whether I should at least try to design a normal day, like everyone else, a very strong feeling came over me. It was in my body and in the room. I was even aware that it was in my neighborhood. Then It vibrated a message to me. I was very aware that it wasn't from me or an imagined or a projected me. This voice was its own intelligence, and it permeated everything.

"If you choose to proceed, please find a same time and place to sit every day. We will assist."

Okay, I thought. *I can do that.* I literally had nothing else to do. My recent divorce settlement had provided just enough cushion in my bank account so that I didn't immediately have to return to the upside-down world – making a living, as they say. I began wondering, *Should I go back to school? Maybe join a choir? I know. I'll schedule a trip to...*

"No thinking." The frequency spiked beneath my skin. "Stay here with no thought. Stay with your body. Practice this everyday – same time, same place."

Sure. Um, okay. Let's see, breath. Focus on my breath. I recalled and practiced a few mechanical meditation tips that I'd learned in healing school. That was it. Perfect. Breathe in. Breathe out. No thought. It's how everybody does it, right?

This went on for about five minutes before I started thinking about a grocery list. I decided that it was a good-enough first effort to impress this new, inner coach. I never liked the group meditation part of healing school, anyway, because I noticed that it didn't work the same for me as it did for others – an echo of learning disabilities from long ago.

Sometimes, when I was without thought in the group, even for a few seconds, I felt stirrings of energy that would activate in my heart, on my palms, and on the bottoms of my feet. While everyone else was routinely guided to, "Bring the energy down from the crown chakra," my experience was one of, "Uh-oh, the magnetic force is pooling on the bottoms of my feet again." I knew what could happen. It wanted to surge all the way up and out through my spine and spontaneously sound out through my throat and widely stretched mouth. This occurred a few times at home, but I told no one. I barely acknowledged it myself. Why would I allow it in a large group? It didn't care one bit that I was still painfully shy around people.

It could easily turn into a string of strange, foreign-sounding words, dancing hand gestures, and the primal groans of a feared and forgotten fem-dragon from long ago. It was as if She was waking up and crying out to the universe – to be heard and to be seen, after what seemed like an eternity of captivity. For me, it was the familiar foreplay that if unrestrained would lead to full-body, spine-arching, brilliant explosions. Long after the dust settled, there would be a stillness that would fill my body and the air, along with a resolute purpose and a clear intent to fly. Still, I was quite certain that it was not ready for prime time. These sounds were not only sure to disturb the polite air in the classroom, but they would more than likely traumatize my fellow students.

While I knew that many might name this "Kundalini," a nice enough word, I am also ultra-aware of the panic that ensues when one can't find a well-behaved place to catalog a certain out-of-bounds ferocity and wildness. This force refuses to be contained in the civilized world, let alone in a four-syllable word. So it was me who seized control and squelched it before it embarrassed us and everyone. You're welcome.

A week or so went by with a similar progression of five to fifteen minutes of the no-thought exercises. Nothing happened. Damned those expectations! This was the point that I began to talk out loud to the resonant voice.

"Yeah, so did I just imagine that? Last week? You, or It, encouraging me to do this? I feel stupid now." I was never one who needed to develop a spiritual practice to feel spiritual. Nor do I need to be taken away in a straitjacket. "Seriously, what's the point of this?" *Sigh.* No response. *There goes that crazy imagination of mine.*

At this point, even though I felt vulnerable and awkward, I consciously noted an intriguing switch-up in my relationship with this Intelligence. In the past, it seemed that it was always other beings and circumstances that were happening *to* me. Now I was being asked to open and invite something to exist *through* me. So often I could literally feel the power of it pressing against my back and at the bottoms of my feet, ready to punch through the locked, flimsy plywood gates that I was convinced kept me safe from the unexplained. I knew that sooner or later it had to give up on me and find someone else to rush through, annihilating yet another life built upon the surface of sand.

Another few weeks went by with little to no revelation, but for some reason, I kept with the schedule. Even though I couldn't articulate it, I felt that I was moving in the right direction.

The date was October 31, 1998. I had become more proficient in resting within the nothingness. The previous day, I had purchased the bags of sugar bombs that I knew many kids would be requesting on this All Hallows' Eve. I staged the assortment of candy in a large bowl by the front door. In another universe, this would have been amusing. Despite my active engagement with unseen cosmic frequencies, I continued to be the programmed automaton acting out the Hallmark-prescribed, social customs of the day. On this morning, however, as I sat in my same-time, same-place laboratory, something happened. I had quickly emptied any thought, and almost immediately felt the growing, enveloping vibrations that delivered a long-awaited message.

"Bring your attention to the womb, your womb. Rest here, and feel the pregnant possibilities."

I followed through with the guidance and felt a cavernous, echoey feeling inside. Soon something clicked and began to open, or blossom, within my body and consciousness. It slowly filled me up. Initially it was a few and then it grew into thousands of buzzing bees. I lost touch with any shred of a thinking mind, as it simply evaporated into no-time, or way-too-fast time.

Without warning, this loud vibration shoved me further inward – into the center of the hive. I was completely one with the primal resonant feelings of an ancient-future movement in my body and being. It flashed, and it thundered, pounding me into the center of my Self and straight into the genesis of what felt like a cosmic-source hurricane of sound. But this full-body concert didn't culminate just yet. It kept rising in frequency and power to the point that I at once imploded and exploded simultaneously. Pure cosmic sound burst through my lungs and out my mouth, bellowing the sounds of galaxies and stars. I was feeling and giving voice to far more than my tiny human self.

If someone had been passing by my window that day, I'm sure they would've heard the last utterance and breath of life from the lungs and belly of a dying 3D human. It continued coursing through my body with its mysterious, fiery resolve until I was finally released. Somehow I understood and accepted the quiet, unexplained nothingness.

I came to inside the hum of a mother's lullaby. The nurturing was divine. I had no sense of time, but eventually I was able to stand up and move slowly. There was an undertone of vibration – a few bees still hanging close to the hive. I recall walking about with a hypersensitivity and awareness of carpet under my feet. Even the air seemed to be aware – passing through the suggestion of skin, muscle, and bone. I simply observed it. Perhaps I watered a plant, but mostly I sat and stared into space with little to no thought; it was all feeling.

Eventually, a few thoughts returned. I wondered whether I'd lost my mind or, at the very least, whether I'd been properly reassembled after the beehive exploded.

Later that afternoon, I sensed a nudge of an invitation to return to my laboratory – my little experiment with fully trusting a communicating energy that felt like the Source of All. Forgetting all about the impending kids-and-candy holiday of persistent interruption – forgetting the outer world completely – I sat back down in my office chair and began to tearfully speak out loud to It.

"I am feeling... no words to match this. I don't want to go crazy. I'm not afraid... really. Confused. I'm drifting. I know this... this energy, but I don't understand *this*."

"Return to the womb." It said quite clearly. So I did. Just the way I had been guided. I easily felt my way back to the frequency of what they referred to as the womb. The vibrations began increasing again almost immediately. It filled me with an indescribable love. My body rocked back and forth in ecstasy for what felt like an eternity.

There was no advance warning or feeling indicator for what occurred next. A brilliant gold-white light flashed and pierced the room. I recall the extreme stinging sensation behind my tightly shut eyes and the center of my forehead. It seemed I would certainly be blinded. All I could do was weep. This had nothing to do with feeling afraid or crying out in self-pity; it was something that was too beautiful to contain. It became so large that I fell out of my chair and onto my knees. I continued to weep until it let up enough for me to find a thought, and with that thought, I cried out,

"Oh god... oh god, oh god, dear god... my heart. *Please help!* This must be... death."

An endless stream of my guttural responses to Infinity transitioned into silence. Finally, after a slight shift in composure by returning upright in the chair, I found my words, "What do I name this Love? I need to know. Please." I said it with a tone and resolve I had not previously known within my being. There was no hesitation as it responded with a decisive force. Pictures rapidly burst into my mind's eye – just like when I was a child in the sandbox. Except this time, there was far more light, far more acceleration, and far more pressure in the center of my head.

The light incinerated my eyes as the pictures and movie clips rushed by so rapidly that I could not make out any single frame. Then it abruptly stopped. It zoomed in on the face of an exquisitely, beautiful young man standing before me. And it stopped again.

I gasped and cried out from the sheer intensity, as well as the deep pain and recognition of this presence. I knew it well. This exquisite heart before me had rushed in with the force of a thousand waterfalls of firelight – with the singular intention to blend with my own little embers. I cried out again, as if it were my final breath, "Please, please. What do I name you? This Love? This Presence? I feel you. I know you. I love you [weeping]... no words."

There was a very long pause. I composed myself, and naturally rocked to and fro with the energies. Soon, in its own perfect rhythm within our cocreated song, I heard-felt the response very clearly, "Beloved." He boomed and radiated into my consciousness and every cell of my physicality, "I AM here." With this, I wept even more. I again lost my capacity to think, process, and find a suitable stopping place in which to file the experience or the Presence. I was aware that there was a distinct choice. If I resisted the oncoming force of these searing currents of light, I would have succumbed to an indescribable, fiery pain. If I continued to surrender, it would be terrifying, but I knew that I would survive. It truly is the strangest dichotomy – simultaneously experiencing total ecstasy and total terror of the unknown. This is how I know to this day when I am being stretched into more – when Love is too much, as if it will annihilate you.

Who, if I cried out, would hear me among the
angels' hierarchies?
And even if one of them pressed me suddenly
against his heart:
I would be consumed in that overwhelming existence.
For beauty is nothing but the beginning of terror,
which we are still just able to endure,
and we are so awed because it serenely disdains
to annihilate us.
Every angel is terrifying.
And so I hold myself back and swallow
the call-note of my dark sobbing.
Ah, whom can we ever turn to in our need?
Not angels, not humans, and already the
knowing animals are aware
that we are not really at home
in our interpreted world.[13]

~ RAINER MARIA RILKE

The Beloved Presence was *here* – inside and out. It did not communicate through the interpreted world. I refer to a poem by Rilke that I'd come across many years later and would've never understood before this event. This Presence communicated through the soul – through the resonant language of a vibrational field. It clearly resounded from within every organ, every hair, and every molecule of my body. It informed me that I needed to know and accept how beautiful I am, how beautiful every human is – every one. He continued with his ecstatic, cellular singing, informing me that even though it seemed so, I – and no one else – had ever actually been alone at any point in this life. I didn't think it possible, but with this, I wept even more. It felt as if even my guts would shake loose and willingly pour out as an offering to the altar of overwhelming Love.

Then the doorbell rang.

There was still a faraway part of me that remembered it was Halloween, but there was absolutely nothing I could do. I became completely absorbed in the frequency and fell into the nothingness. Later, I awoke in the dark on the living room couch.

I worked it out later that I must've been there for at least a day and a half. I couldn't move. I felt weak as I drifted in and out of consciousness. At one point, I opened my eyes and realized that I was still on the couch. A few mundane thoughts passed through me – like the tones of a nearby cricket – oblivious to my event and still gently riding the in and out of my breath. Thoughts occasionally surfaced within my local consciousness. *Do I need to go to the bathroom. Drink water? Do I call someone? Who would I call? How can I explain this to another human being? Am I dying? I'm pretty sure I'm dying, and that's okay, really. I'm good with that.*

On what felt like the third day, I opened my eyes and felt somewhat stronger. Sitting up, I realized that there was someone who might be able to help me define this. Even though I felt weak, I very carefully made my way to the kitchen and found the phone. David would know.

I called David, a PhD psychologist and my personal therapist, who was also one of the teachers at my healing school. I didn't have to explain much. He seemed to know more than what I could articulate, and this not only seemed deserving of his attention, but he also created a sacred space in which to listen and advise. "No need to explain further. Continue to rest," he said. "Get yourself some water, and rest. Know that this is truly a gift. We'll talk soon."

Excuse me sir, could it be I've lost my mind?
'Cause your voice brings tears to my eyes.
He said no, but you walked through my door today,
And all those tears, in your eyes,
I'll kiss away.[14]

~ E. MEYER (LYRICS)

VI

Beloved

A Presence and a Song

—⦿—

When the gentle hunter shot me
and left me in all my weakness,
in the arms of love
my soul fell
and being charged with new life
I have changed in such a way
That My Beloved is for me
and I am for my Beloved.[15]

~ TERESA OF AVILA

The next time I awoke, it felt like afternoon. I got up and mindlessly shuffled about. My stomach was cramping with hunger, and I noticed that my nearby pitcher of water was empty. I had no memory of drinking it. I thought it would be wise to eat something. Nothing sounded good, so I rummaged around and found some stale crackers. It felt strange in my mouth, but I managed to chew and swallow a bit of the sawdust texture.

I stared in confusion at the giant bowl of mini candy bars. I hadn't noticed any more knocking or doorbells on Halloween, but still I knew my condo community. There would've been many of the usual ghouls, goblins, and superheroes clamoring to receive the treats, especially after working so hard to transform their identities into something more, better, prettier, or scarier than their everyday selves.

"Sorry," I mumbled, feeling the irony of my epic de-identification with masks and images over the course of my All Hallows' Eve.

I walked back into the living room, wondering whether I should just lie down again. My eyes rested on a dusty, stringed zither instrument that I had on my shelf. I think a fan had given it to me at a show, but since it wasn't tuned and I didn't know how to play it anyway, it had become a decoration on the bookshelf. On top of the speaker next to the shelf was a dust rag – probably abandoned at a point when my attention had been diverted to something far more interesting than housework.

I picked up the rag. How could I have let things get so dusty? I bumped the instrument clumsily and four or five notes loudly rang out into the room. The sound struck me to my core, and I froze. The notes resonated deeply and decisively within my body, and they did not fade as the strings stopped vibrating. In fact, the notes continued to move and resound within my hollowed-out body. They clearly had an agenda of their own. I backed up from the bookshelf and held tightly onto the edge of the couch. The pressure continued to rise and showed no signs of stopping until I understood that action was required.

Instinct moved me toward my electric piano – yet another decorative piece. I dusted it off and began a process of locating my memory banks to recall how the keyboard worked. My brain was different. Everything was different. An analogy to help explain the sensory experience of finding and re-activating the old thought files again might be something like being blindfolded with earplugs, taken to a remote and unfamiliar location, released, and then told that I was free to find my way back home. My mind was confused because a linear memory of my transport to these new landscapes wasn't available, and there were no breadcrumbs in sight.

Therefore, there was no logical retracing of steps to get back. But, did I want to go back? Or was the impulse just a rat-in-the-maze habit to return to the familiar? I surrendered again. I've always been one to admit when I had lost my way.

I allowed my body to lead me through this freeform, open-ended dance. It was not unlike the experiences I'd had in the past of waking up and speaking or singing foreign words while my hands danced – in perfect tune with the energy. Instead of following the usual commands from the usual part of my brain, energy moved and responded to my feeling aware-ness in seamless and graceful ways. I could see and understand more in each new moment. It felt as if I was being given an opportunity to engage and practice using a once cordoned-off part of my being. It was like learn-ing a new form of communication in a total-immersion, interdimensional language course. It seemed that while I was sleeping, I had slipped into a vast sea – the forbidden, watery parts of my consciousness. It was thrilling, but at the same time, I sensed that I'd broken the law – almost like *The Matrix* police would be arriving soon to arrest me, punish me, and send me back to the designated, left-brained box.

When I spoke about this watery reality as a child, I was hushed. Apologies were quickly made on my behalf for pointing out the obvious and true. Eventually, most children come to agree with the lie, that there is no water, where real feelings swim and thrive. Yet there I was with the desire to feel and translate ITs purpose for inviting me back in to recall my honesty and innocence and to expose every lie that I had previously bought into.

It had been a while since I'd played piano, only because it made me very sad and guilty that I had not kept up with it. There were stacks of music books nearby – all of my old standards and favorites that I loved to sing way back when. Of course I'd sung with a variety of bands for over twelve years at that point, and I didn't need a piano to sing cover songs. I had the blessing of having brilliantly skilled musicians on stage with me to accomplish that.

I finally got the old keyboard powered up and selected a piano sound that I could temporarily live with. There wasn't the time or attention to focus on the mechanics of tools and buttons. I sat down, took a deep breath, and sort of turned the faucet on. It was an invitation to the collection of notes that were still whirling inside and all around my dining-meditation-music room – lovingly held in a sort of soft, pink-colored sphere. I could feel that the sound wanted to move through my humming throat, down my arms, and on to the keys. As soon as I found and played the sequence of chords by ear, the tones refilled my heart, and then my hands moved to the next progression of chords. After only slight hesitation, as if waiting for their cue, out danced the lyrics – like a string of ballerinas who were poised and proud to contribute to the song.

Thankfully, nearby was a coffee-stained chord chart for reference. I needed to match where my hands landed on the keys, with the corresponding letter chords and dimensions. I felt unprepared for the task, as I had only known sheet music that my mom had taught me to read years ago. I scratched out a quasi-musical sort of shorthand on a nearby notepad. If I got lost again, I could find my way back to this place – this lovely, lovely place. Soon my feeling efforts coalesced into a very long and beautiful song, aptly named "Beloved." It was only then, after about an hour and a clear sense of completion, that I noticed the magnetic, pressure-cooker insistence to move and create had stopped. The first five notes of the song are an exact match to the notes that rang out from the stringed-instrument on the shelf. The rest of the song arrived in a timeless blur.

I had both written and cowritten a few original songs before, during a time when I was attempting to learn guitar, but nothing like this had ever happened to me before. Two of these songs had been poems that I struggled to find melodies for. This song, "Beloved," and many more to come, had pressed me to receive and capture it in lyrics, chords, and melodies all at once. Once I adapted to the method of delivery, it was easy, but I had a little trouble keeping up with how fast and furiously it came.

Later, I played "Beloved" for my dear friend, James. He was moved to tears and could not stop encouraging me to record and share it. I reminded him that I'd quit music – months ago. The whole scene just wasn't right for me anymore. I was moved by his reaction and his insistence to think about it. So I did. I found that the motivating force within me to move ahead with recording – this song and many more to come – was that this music might help others feel the Presence and perhaps inspire them to find their own inner roadmaps too. If that were the case, there was no question. I had to – even if there was just a chance it could happen.

Obviously, James was another human angel who was present in my life for many reasons, which thankfully included nudging me in this direction. I'm very grateful. I don't believe I would've chosen to go in this direction on my own. For me, it was just too deeply personal. Thus, it would've stayed inside the boundary of my own heart.

As soon as I tentatively agreed to record the song professionally, mind-boggling synchronicities quickly connected me to a "producer that I absolutely had to meet" – Larry Mitchell. Larry heard "Beloved" for the first time in 1999, in Solana Beach, California, and offered to produce it for free. He added that if I didn't love it, I could still walk away with my recorded song and find another professional to help when I was ready. Of course I loved it. And by then, I had a growing body of scribed songs that I never planned to write, but they came to me anyway – musical compositions that arrived in colored spheres of light – beautiful packages of energy that I unraveled over hours. I should note that it felt that my human consciousness and perspective was alive in the spheres. It was a collaboration with my Self and more.

More than one song would be delivered from the colored spheres at once, so some pieces, including "Beloved," were multiple songs fused in to ten-to-fifteen minute-long melodies. Larry helped me to pull them apart and create radio-friendly, appropriate-length songs. Another anomaly in the way these songs arrived was that I heard instruments and tones that

I have yet to find exact matches for in this world. I can only describe them as a background of electronic sounds with a sort of ethereal, tribal intensity – a fascinating blend. But poor Larry – I could not properly translate these sounds into words. Still, he blew me away with his production choices in the end.

By the year 2000, I had 1,000 copies of my first CD, *Inevitable*, in the trunk of my car as I headed for Santa Fe, New Mexico. This land made herself known via many dreams towards the end of the century. She beckoned me to come.

Another song on the album appealed to a new Santa Fe friend, Ira Gordon. He was the general manager of my favorite station – KBAC Radio Free, Santa Fe 98.1. I loved this station so much that I played it over the Internet while still a resident of San Diego. It was a wonderful eclectic mix of both known and obscure artists, so I had felt compelled to send an advance copy of my new CD for the station's consideration. After meeting up with Ira in Santa Fe, I was delighted and surprised that he placed the song, "Home," in the station's regular rotation.

Little did anyone know that the songs were dialogs between me and, well, I never knew what to call IT. God was a name that didn't fit – too many versions, too many connotations from the past. Jesus might work, but that identity belonged to a major religion, so it felt exclusionary. While I felt joyful resonance in later reading the great saints and mystics' translations of ecstatic, connected states, these human lives were captured and interpreted mainly through the context of the Catholic Church. I had no such infrastructure, nor did I want it. All I knew was that this Presence didn't belong, and would never belong, to any existing dogma or framework in the interpreted world. I struggled with this for many years to come – how to explain it, to frame it, again and again. But this new era of my life was obviously different, as I was now regularly front facing with the public. I performed these songs at concert venues and churches, as well as nightclubs and bars across the western states – where beers and shots of tequila seemed to increase the confusion about who I was and what these songs were about.

"You have a really pretty voice, but what are you singing about? Your boyfriends? Wait, are you a Christian? It's nice. Hey, do you know any Destiny's Child?"

VII

The Dance Between Two Worlds
This is Amazing… and Impossible

———— ∞ ————

*Your visions will become clear only when you can look
into your own heart. Who looks outside, dreams;
who looks inside, awakes.*

~ CARL JUNG

To this day I am baffled by the series of events that created dozens of original songs, an explosion of writing, poetry, and more. Before this, I had quit music, and quit everything, really. I had no further inspiration to create music or perform or even reconfigure what I wanted to be when I grew up. The predominant feeling was "been there done that" and "nothing new under the sun." I'd emptied myself of any pride of the past or designs for fitting into the future. I was neutral, just sitting inside my womb, when everything changed.

I loved Santa Fe. What came next was exploring and demonstrating the being who I was and perpetually in the act of becoming. I listened; I was always listening to feel and know when to take action, when to sing, when to speak, or when to stay quiet. It was all about continuing to refine and integrate the dance that my Beloved had initiated in a San Diego condo on All Hallows' Eve 1998. I felt and navigated the energy – both honoring my own, as well as the energies of others in my community. Was it okay to be me yet? I regularly imagined what the bridging of my two worlds might look like. Maybe I'm on a stage with a large, enthusiastic crowd seated before me, and I say,

"Over the course of my entire life, I've been visited by spirit beings, angels, and extraterrestrials. They seemed intent on initiating numerous, full-body ecstatic awakenings and resonance teachings. I now see and feel the evolving truth about humanity, our Creator, and the miracles and magic we are capable of manifesting on Earth. And here's a little song I wrote about it…" (The crowd roars with applause and appreciation.)

Hilarious! The Presence had always had a fine sense of humor, but I wasn't laughing – much. It was how I would've loved to introduce my songs on stage, but I didn't feel I could at the time. It was 2001, and even in woo-woo Santa Fe, New Mexico, I remained quite the undercover contactee. Some have asked me why I didn't join up with the growing New Age and UFO communities, as certainly I could find some kind of compatibility there. I explored that, but it's never been the saucers in the sky for me. This is where the group fascination is now, and I understand. But for me, it's always been about the transformational aspect, the activation and evolution of consciousness within. Whenever someone excitedly told me that they'd seen a UFO, my immediate reaction was always, "So cool! Tell me. Tell me, what did you feel?" Most of the time I received a disapproving glance from them with a very clear energetic message, "What the [bleep] does that matter? I *saw* a spaceship!" It seemed that even in the fringe groups, I was weird. Naturally, I backed off.

Perhaps I just haven't met other experiencers like me – yet. Thankfully, in the 1990s, I located others like me in John Mack's book, *Abducted*. I didn't resonate with the title of the book because I never felt that I was abducted, but several of Mack's subjects, and Mack himself, seemed more appreciative of the transformational aspect of contact. To me, the lucid dreams, the visions, and the visits always emphasized, "On the inside, not the outside. We fly direct to your heart and mind." [16]

From the early to mid-2000s, there didn't seem to be a shortage of opportunities for me to sing, even though a few local musicians had initially warned me otherwise. They all seemed to agree from their own experience that Santa Fe didn't welcome original music. I found that to be mostly true, and while I had no big plans or any idea how I might fit into the local business of music, I knew that I could never return to my past of being a human jukebox (one that regurgitated everyone's favorite tunes on command). So I struck a compromise.

I met some truly talented musicians in Santa Fe, and eventually we landed a regular downtown gig at the beautiful and historic La Posada Hotel. Friday nights became a cozy, musical gathering of friends and tourists by the fire – with mainly cello, violin, piano, and guitar. To this day, it remains one of my fondest performance memories by far.

My inspiration from the start was that I'd begin with a repertoire of old standards and slowly introduce my original songs into the mix. It seemed to work. One evening as I sang out to the crowd – later referred to by the regulars as "Friday Night Church" – I realized that over time my repertoire had shifted from 100 percent to 10 percent cover songs. Yes, I was welcomed to sing 90 percent of the night with my original music – songs birthed from colored balls of light. It happened on its own, and I couldn't have felt more delighted and fulfilled.

I am eternally grateful for those gatherings. I very much needed the care and familial support in my life. Many of these old, Santa Fe friends, and even the passing-through friends, had no idea how important they were in helping me to keep my sanity and maintain a sense of value in the world.

It was in the midst of all this that I met my longtime friend, soul-partner, and Mayan priest, Eduardo Griego. Truth be told, it was the Mayan priest part that originally got my attention. One of the audience members whispered in my ear that I might want to meet this man, as he had spent much time in Guatemala studying Mayan science. This triggered something huge within – the memory of that pivotal message delivered in

December 1995 from the elaborately and colorfully dressed Mesoamerican leader, the one who seemed quite focused on delivering the most urgent of messages to me in my living room – projecting images in the center of my head, insisting that I needed to "get on with the work." On the band's next break, I introduced myself to Eduardo. Later, it proved to be an important meeting and alliance.

These visions, visits, and lucid dreams had never made linear sense to me when they occurred, and I recorded them in my journals in a raw and unattached way. After that, I simply trusted. I had always been guided to push past the need for comparisons and immediate definition in terms of the existing models and frames of the world. The Loving Intelligence was very strongly consistent about this: hold it all very lightly, and trust that it will be understood in the end. At the same time, I frequently asked myself, "Could I be nuts?" I mean, I'm well aware that a lot of this sounds like what you might hear walking down the halls of a mental institution or more often today from the disenfranchised and homeless on the streets in Anytown, U.S.A. I always came back to the fact that during high Visitor-activity times, I've held some highly technical jobs in the areas of extreme-multitasking, project management, executive assistance to CEOs, accounting, video and audio editing, and copywriting – and with Eduardo, running a digital media production business for years. I wore every hat. Can crazy people do that?

These represent long stretches of consciously dismissing my heart consciousness, and the rest of my brain, so that I too could focus on what we're all taught to focus on here. I can do it – and quite well – but I can't ignore the fact that under these circumstances, my soul gradually withers. In our culture, it's important to keep these things compartmentalized; however, it's never worked for me.

It's like having your left eye patched when you're born, and everyone in your community wears the patch too. Don't question it. If it causes discomfort – physically, mentally, or emotionally – we have medicine to help you forget that something is off-balance or missing. And life goes on, right? Suck it up.

Let's say someone's left-eye patch just falls off one day, and after a time of adjustment, this person can suddenly see – way better. It's too amazing not to tell people about it! Everyone in the community calls her crazy and refuses to acknowledge the fact that she's experiencing joy and wonder with her new, illuminating discoveries – not only about herself, but also about the human race. Could it be that our Creator provided us with another eye? Why were we never told about this? Why do people shut down or avoid her when she speaks of it? She learns to put the patch back on when at school or work; otherwise, she won't be able to survive in the world. Still, she loves spending time alone, practicing using both eyes – seeing the many more dimensions of life.

Not only was I strengthening my ability to de-code the Visitor's frequency-language, but I also grew in my ability to discern the dissonant tones of the egoic, or programmed, mind as well. It had a sort of middle-management demand for immediate meaning. The linear mind continued to insist that the anomalies be sorted, addressed with existing knowledge, and quickly filed away in the safety of an old, familiar file folder. I simply acknowledged this pressing, mental need before the anxiety had its way by calmly explaining to the panicky middle manager, "Relax. Something's in the air. It could be that we're reorganizing and redefining our roles here… maybe the entire organization."

Journal Entry: December 13, 2001

I woke up in my dream aware that I was dreaming (lucid), watching a CAD-3D computer screen while getting a download of technical and spiritual info – one and the same. It was all about energy, creation, and how we are what we create – no separation. Nothing is outside. During the teaching, I felt and knew this within my being – that I was the knowledge that was being downloaded.

[Note: While I'm immersed in the heightened state of lucidity, it makes perfect sense. When I write it here in the journal, I'm very aware how nonsensical it sounds.]

In 2002, Eduardo was my guide and teacher through my Mayan Fire Path journey in Guatemala, which culminated in my initiation at the Grand Plaza in Tikal. It was a surprisingly empty plaza, considering it was the Mayan New Year of Waxakib B'aatz. At the close of Eduardo's heart-full guidance through my small but potent ceremony, I was moved to climb to the top of the Pyramid of the Sun and commune directly with my Creator. I felt the power of the Mayan leader within as I stood overlooking the empty Grand Plaza of Tikal, and I spoke out loud with a strong yet simple clarity.

"This experience, this life, has been amazing, difficult, and perfect. I am filled with the many memories and blessings here. I am filled with abundant gratitude for all. I'm stating now that I make myself completely available to the service of Love, the service of the Great Mother, and the Father of Creation, but I am unwilling to be framed in this life as a Mayan priest(ess) or framed into anything from the past. Show me who I am in the center of now. Show me how I can best serve as we move into this rapidly changing reality."

Of course most of us had been exposed to the media's dire, cataclysmic framing of the Mayan 2012 End of the Long Count calendar, whether you were aware of Mayan science or not. The Maya simply reported through their calendar that it was the end of a larger cosmic cycle. It was a good thing. On to the new! I felt that it was an important marker in time, but it was quite clear to me that the most important marker to uncover was within each individual's consciousness. In other words, it was up to each of us to locate it and let it light the way of our everyday footsteps.

Through the next several years, I continued to receive, record, and perform more music. It arrived in similar ways as it had before. The next two CDs to come, also produced by Larry Mitchell, seemed to have more pieces from my human view – as an awakening or blending being on Earth – with a few other direct messages from the Mother, or Gaia, sprinkled about. While I was dedicated to stay true to the musical poetry as it arrived in my consciousness, many people thought I was making a mistake. They thought that if I shifted to become a more popular musical artist, I would more than likely be quite successful. This, I had no interest in. I had no worldly goals. I was following an inner energetic guidance that I trusted implicitly. However, from time to time I questioned my sanity with these choices, as the money aspect of living in the world wasn't always easy. While performing and selling music provided some sustenance, I still had to figure out how to attract more while remaining true to, or integral with, my heart.

Eduardo and I made money by doing television and radio advertising with our digital media business – always promoting a more conscious and integral approach long before conscious marketing was a thing. We were committed and ready to guide clients into a more benevolent, less-manipulative approach to advertising. We had a few great clients with decent budgets who were on board with the vision. Our heart-conscious ideas worked for them beautifully. However, the majority of our clients weren't quite ready to make that leap. The interesting thing was that most agreed with our philosophy, but in the end, they chose the usual, way-its-always-been approach. Truth was too risky for them on all levels.

Eventually I had to supplement my income by returning to the corporate business world. I could still adapt easily in just about any kind of office and administrative work. Most times, it was very difficult for me to lock into a rigid nine-to-five schedule, but the Presence within provided the energy and fortitude required, along with the wisdom to know that it was temporary. I must say, though, I took issue with the term "temporary" being used to describe more than a decade and a half of time, but I can see that it might all be a matter of dimensional perspective. Basically, I did what I had to do to keep going, but soon I began to notice that I was growing tired, very tired. I honestly didn't know how much longer I could hang in there.

Mainly I found myself waiting for an elusive something that I couldn't explain but knew was occurring that would lead to something quite spectacular – for all humanity. I was informed by my Visitors throughout my entire life, in many different ways, that there was going to be a huge shift in human consciousness. In the meantime, I became a master at patience.

The one constant in this life has been the split in consciousness. In one form or another, I straddled the chasm between who I discovered I truly am and who I appear to be in the world – for the sake of consistency. The 3D identities were simple enough to try on, wear for a time, and exchange for new when it was appropriate and necessary. It was the "who I truly am" that continued to be wordless and difficult to translate to people, especially when the overtones from beyond the bandwidth would not support nesting – finding a frame and identity that would fit nicely and comfortably within the world. I knew who I was through frequency or resonant identification, but since this had no visibility or value in the smaller bandwidth, knowing who I was continued to be a lonely secret that always distanced me from others.

For sanity's sake, I did my best to show up for my regular meditations. I practiced the form given to me from within, just before the Beloved event. It had always felt so empowering. Still, I recall one of my teachers in healing school informing me that when someone or something started to communicate with me during meditation, I was doing it wrong. *Sigh.*

Journal Entry: April 3, 2003, Notes from Meditation

I was exploring my lifelong series of questions and doubts around the purpose of my life, etc. Yesterday I saw a quote from a spiritual author – stating that the soul requires "specializing efforts." It had come at the exact moment – before I fell into yet another pit of despair. They were saying that our biggest problem here on Earth is that we don't pick just one thing to become exceptional at. I'm aware that I've become a Jill of all trades here – simply to survive.

I prayed and centered – asking for help and fully expected it, but I didn't know how the guidance would get through my pain. Eventually, the fog lifted, and I was at peace. Then the pointed question they like to ask from time to time came through again. "Imagine you have ten million dollars easily at your disposal. What would you do with that freedom?"

It's always been a great exercise for me. It cuts away the bullshit of everyday life – of mainly trying to fit in with some kind of moneymaking product or service so that people will buy it and you can eat. Ugh! But with this exercise, there was no more "making it fit" with ten million in the bank. It's a good method to find out more of what the soul wants. I truly had to weed through some crap that had gathered around this topic. Excellent. Precisely what they were after. I sifted through, realizing that I had once again tripped myself up with belief systems around music and the music biz – so much so that I had lost touch with the essence of what I love. I then found myself in a resting place after these observations. Out of this peace came a question.

"What if the one thing for you is, perhaps, being a translator, a translator for frequency?"

Yes! My whole body and being lit up like a Christmas tree. I didn't know exactly what it meant or what that looked like, but it sure turned on the passion switch in me! The next thing I knew I was being taken through a kind of life review – the angels, the dreams, the visions, and the messages had been so consistent throughout my life. I can feel the very core of my being vibrate with excitement at the idea of being an interdimensional translator. They've dropped these hints before.

So out of this nothing place, that one question had lit me on fire again – the fire that I had lost sight and sense of because of the worldly influence to fit into existing boxes. I will do my best now to interpret what came next. It never seems to be linear. Rather, I feel and see with higher senses and allow them to fall into patterns that I can assign words to – words that are required for pencil and paper or to share with another individual. Translation!

In the visions, I was shown little books that I had written. A few of them go with my musical CDs. Each chapter is a song. The music was never intended to stand by itself. The books help to bridge. There are other little books too – some from the past and some from now (the "past" meaning an autobiographical-type account of my journey; the other books were real-time recordings of my messages from these angel beings).

"You could call the publishing company, Gold Nugget Press." It had a tongue-in-cheek feel and was a very deliberate return of consciousness to the frequency of gold that they say is where all of my answers and knowings come from. I am told even these hills outside of my window are filled with gold and to practice resonating with them. I dreamt of these hills and was guided to move here. I never questioned it, and we did so. It turned out that it was absolutely true. The hills were full of gold, but the technology had been too expensive to extract it.

I always knew that these journal writings would have tremendous value to me someday. I only began to record these experiences and knowings because I had no one to talk with about it. I was so different from anybody I knew, including my own family. I understand now that there are many, many people on this planet who sense beyond what they are taught to sense. I hope to meet some of them someday. For now, my angelic helpers have always been my friends, family, business associates, and creative collaborators.

The journal entry went on to detail the outline of four books, and emphasized that there was another whole body of work yet to come. This proved to be quite accurate, but it wouldn't occur for another few years.

I'm not sure you can be more humbled and brought to your knees as much as I have in my life while still remaining alive, productive, and sane. I am human through and through, but throughout the Visitor's dedicated awakening program, there have been significant changes to my being that feel larger, or more than what we had been taught was human here on Earth.

Because of these bioenergetic events, I seem to have more awareness about the split that has occurred in other people too, as well as the specific fears and defense mechanisms that keep them locked in the past. When someone asks me sincerely and honestly about how they might re-establish their own whole consciousness and capacities, I am able to hear their Soul's tones and see their designs for life as a "new whole human" on Earth – inspirations that have mostly been suppressed. I seem to have a larger-bandwidth view, just as the Intelligence in which I resonantly commune with has a larger view than I do.

One of the most important messages that I offer for humanity now is that you naturally contain – within your body and being – everything that you need to awaken and remember who you are, and this is very much present now. It initiates through the feeling-heart network that awakens and extends from inside and expands out far beyond the known bandwidth. It is here that your natural Self resides and is able to surf multiple dimensions of consciousness.

Be that as it may, there are not many who truly want this. They might speak of wanting it, but very few are willing to break the hypnotic spell of life as it's always been in order to peel off the masks and clothing of conditioning. I believe another whole book could be written about cult mentality, deprogramming, and even addiction as analogies to describe the current state of collective consciousness.

But I'm getting ahead of myself. At this point, even I had not fully grokked the possibilities.

VIII

Life Unfolding
Adapting to Synchronicity

—∞—

We do not create our destiny; we participate in its unfolding.
Synchronicity works as a catalyst
toward the working out of that destiny.[17]

~ David Richo, PhD

In 2004 I had a dream that led me directly to the prolific author-channel Robert Shapiro. The Visitors presence spoke to me in the dream, pointing me to an unnamed man who would guide me through a very integral phase of my life. The word "Sedona" was woven throughout the dream messages and that I could easily find him "by way of Arizona."

Oh, c'mon! This had turned a bit too New Agey for my taste. My life may sound like an open, New Age book at this point, but I never identified with this category or label. On the other hand, I'd already had too many lessons to count about the suspension of judgment – letting go of how things sound or appear through the lens of the intellect alone. I remained neutral and allowed the energy to inform me of what I needed to know when I needed to know it.

Over the next few days, I thought about jumping in the car and driving to Sedona. I wanted to see whether I could uncover more about this mysterious dream message in person. *No.* The feeling answer was clear, so I let it go. I suppose I was looking for a reason to escape. Eduardo and I had just moved to Taos, New Mexico. There was still so much unpacking to do, which I dislike very much. I have moved too many times in my life to count.

It was a few days later, while working my way through the remaining stacks of boxes, when I reached for the next big plastic container – a heavy one filled with books. I popped the plastic lid off, and a magnetic energy struck me like a resolute wave. It filled my body with the same vibrational energy that the Visitors arrive with. Obviously I knew it well, and I knew from hundreds of similar experiences that this pressing energy was an indicator of something important. Naturally, I stopped, sat down, and listened.

On this occasion, along with the loving heart energy and the usual feeling-pictures in my mind's eye, an automatic action occurred without thought. This was happening more often now. I would simply become aware that I was already physically moving and doing at some point within the activity. In this case, I had already picked up and opened the book that had been sitting on the very top – before my local consciousness popped back in. I had no memory of purchasing, receiving, or even reading this book. It was brand-new to me. The name of the book was *Council of Creators*, and it was written by Robert Shapiro.

As my eyes drifted down the page, I was energetically struck again by the publisher's name and address in Arizona. I quickly went to the Internet, and not surprisingly, Sedona factored in. The publisher also had a well-known monthly magazine called, *The Sedona Journal of Emergence!*, and later I found out that this publishing company was originally established in Sedona, Arizona. Was this author the one I was being guided to reach out to?

I tried to find his contact info but there was none – except through the publisher. I phoned and left a message on their voicemail, asking to speak to the author, Robert Shapiro. All of this occurred within the magnetic energy. I don't even know exactly what I said. Just like the captivating tones of the songs that wanted to be scribed six years earlier, once I took the action it wanted, the energy was satisfied and then dissipated. Soon I forgot all about it. Weeks went by before I received a return phone call.

It's a simple unfolding when things are meant to be. Robert Shapiro and I conversed for over two hours on the telephone. As strange as it sounds, even though we didn't actually know each other, it felt as if we had a tremendous amount of catching up to do. The energy generated from this meeting fed and greatly nurtured my soul.

At the time, Eduardo and I were working with a video production crew for a local Santa Fe documentary. I was a subject in the film as well. The woman producing it was an ET contactee, and the topic revolved around female experiencers of the benevolent kind. I had the inspiration to fly to Hawaii (where Robert Shapiro was at the time) and, in context of the film, interview the beings that he connected with. It made sense to me. A great deal of his material revolved around messages from ETs. Why not ask them for their view, through Robert, about the phenomenon of contact? I was game. So was Robert.

I wanted to pinch myself. Was this really happening? There I was, on the top of a high-rise Honolulu apartment building, speaking to Robert and his entourage of ETs and natural-world entities. I was both excited and nervous. In the end, one of the more well-known cosmic, and boisterous entities, Zoosh, spoke through Robert and basically stated,

"There are plenty of documentaries out there on the subject already. How does adding one more of these ET-UFO programs truly help? The real question in this moment is, when are you going to begin your channeling work?"

"Yes, well, I've been asked this before," I responded shyly.

"Then maybe it's time!" Zoosh bellowed enthusiastically. "When will you begin?"

Robert didn't know this at the time, but it was the exact same question that Darryl Anka's counterpart, Bashar, had posed almost twenty years earlier. Wow. There it was again. Just as I felt when Bashar reminded me of these dormant skills, I still noticed my reluctance to join up with the New Age category of "channeler." I knew instinctively that because humans were evolving, this entire way of accessing spirit was evolving as well. I was open to the idea that I might be a different kind of channeler, but I had no words to elaborate further.

My very first experience of sitting before a channeler had occurred because a persuasive friend invited me to see one back in the early 1980s. I was very uncomfortable with it all, as I had sensed the clear, energetic markers of deception. It wasn't for me, so I excused myself before it was complete. Today I chuckle at this memory, in light of being a lifetime contactee and essentially *talking* to unseen intelligence over the course of my entire life. It still fascinates me that even though I'm receiving messages from beyond the world as we know it, I wasn't fully on board with the existing containers, methodologies, and categories for this phenomenon. Instinctually, I knew there would be a future reality in which I would fit more comfortably with all this. One day it would all make sense. It had to.

Beginning in the mid-1980s and up through the twenty-first century, I met well-known channels Kevin Ryerson, Darryl Anka, Robert Shapiro, Lee Carroll, Ken Carey, and more in the most serendipitous of ways. As previously described, the magnetic energies notified me first and then synchronistically drew me to where they were. Each connection generated a profound magnetic response within my body – sometimes to the point that I was completely unable to move. I had no word explanations for any of it. I simply trusted the natural process and the strongly felt guidance that it was important we meet.

Author and spiritual teacher Byron Katie was even a part of my life. In the late 1970s and early 1980s, she would come to my father and step-mom's house in Barstow, California, for their Course in Miracles meetings. Sometimes I sat at the table and other times on the periphery. I liked her and rather enjoyed hearing her stretch to find appropriate analogies, parables, and metaphors to express herself. It made me giggle inside to watch another human go through similar motions that I was convinced only I struggled with. Obviously all of that practice paid off for her. I greatly celebrate her service to all the people she has supported and inspired through her empowering books and workshops.

My dad used to warn me that she was the craziest one in the bunch – that we needed to be respectful and patient, as she tended to ramble on about things that made absolutely no sense to the rest of the group. I related very much to this woman, and I must say, it's an honor to find myself assigned to the same, "nutty" category as Katie.

There were more synchronistic meetings with very well-known spiritual teachers as well as unusual encounters with messengers in human form – ones who are performing great work here but do not wish to be known publicly. I'm sure I never would've ended up in the company of any of these extraordinary people if it hadn't been important for me to feel connected to a tribe – a group that felt similarly at odds with the "normal" world while demonstrating a courageous poise and dedication to the spiritual work. And in the case of Robert Shapiro, it extended a little further.

After my visit and interviews with him in 2004, Robert invited me to come to Hawaii to mentor with him. Every cell in my body said, "Yes!" But as usual, I hadn't figured out a way through all the seeming obstacles, limitations, and suggestions that it just wouldn't be possible. At the time, I had no resources to speak of. Every cent I had, including my existing retirement funds, had been poured into capturing and producing songs that had arrived in multidimensional spheres of light.

I returned to the mainland with a lot to ponder. Plus, I needed to complete my work on the *Benevolent ET* documentary. This included an on-camera interview with Dolores Cannon, the prolific author who discovered through hypnosis that far more people were having these interdimensional experiences than previously thought. Dolores was extremely intelligent and one of nicest people you could meet. It was a great honor to spend time with her before she passed in 2014.

When my work was complete on the documentary, I signed up for a conference in Albuquerque on science and shamanic wisdom. It wasn't necessarily a topic that I felt I must know more about. It was the magnetic energy that pulled me into this event. I saw an ad for it. Energy filled me. Monies arrived unexpectedly. I knew I was going. The rest happened effortlessly. This was the exact same feeling-phenomenon that had happened before my meeting with Darryl Anka and Bashar back in 1986. First I'm drawn to a post or flyer, and before my mind has a chance to judge or dismiss it, the magnetics inform my body that I will be attending. It's not mind control; it's body wisdom – a communion that includes the body through a highly loving heart presence. It won't even allow the conditioning to enter and dissuade the soul.

I showed up at the science-wisdom conference and found myself bored and even agitated at the patriarchal approach to it all. This particular conference was advertised to have a distinct emphasis on feminine wisdom. Although it wasn't my strong suit at the time to publicly speak my mind (or should I say, speak my feelings), I felt a growing rage within that I couldn't hold back. I have no recollection of what I said, but it was about actual feminine wisdom being somewhat overlooked in their workshop. If I recall correctly, it didn't go over very well with the all-male "leaders" in the circle. I decided that I'd somehow made an error in judgment by attending this conference, and I made up my mind that I wouldn't return for the final day.

We took a break for refreshments, and I stood alone, still feeling displaced. With an elegant confidence, a beautiful middle-aged woman approached me, meekly excused her intrusion, and asked whether she could speak with me.

"Of course!" I beamed, happy to be connecting with anyone at the conference. People had seemed a bit solitary or kept to their own cliquish groups. We introduced ourselves, and I asked Maggie Boyd whether she was enjoying the conference.

"Well," she said honestly, "Some of it… no, not really. But I liked what you had to say in the circle a little bit ago."

"Oh gosh, I'm sorry about that," I blushed. "I don't know what came over me."

"No apologies necessary," she said. "I believe you may have spoken for several of us. I was feeling a bit disappointed myself. It's just not what I'd expected from reading the brochure. I'm with you. It's time that we all become more conscious of our natural, feminine wisdom. It's about developing and engaging more of our heart consciousness."

Maggie then asked me more about who I am, my work, and what I felt passionately about. I told her about my music, my expanding spiritual work, and that I really saw myself writing a book about my lifetime of mystical experiences – someday. Of course I had spoken all of this in the smoother, sound bite ways that I'd developed over time. Most people, I'd noticed, were unable to keep their eyes from glazing over when I spoke of the consciousness-changing ET contact and evolutionary messages. Maggie was not only aligned and intrigued; she added so much more dimension to our dialog.

At the close of the break, she asked to meet up in Santa Fe for a visit soon, adding that she would be headed back to her home on the East Coast in about a week's time. Of course I agreed, and it was at the close of the day's agenda that she told me an incredible story. Maggie's mother-in-law had been a beloved healer and channel for many years in New York. Before she passed away, she had specifically set aside money to support women who were actively doing and evolving "the work." She asked her daughter-in-law, Maggie, to manage and distribute the funds accordingly, as she would completely trust her future instincts and choices after she was gone.

"Wow, that's an amazing story," I beamed, "How wonderful for you to be in such a fun, fairy godmother position!"

Maggie smiled and said, "Yes. Yes, it is. I look forward to meeting up with you in Santa Fe soon."

A few days later, I was having a cup of tea with Maggie in her Santa Fe apartment. We laughed, told stories, and found that we had a great deal in common. I truly delighted in her company. Toward the end of my visit, as I gathered my things, she blurted out, "I'd like to offer you some financial support to further your work." She paused for a moment and smiled, "Or rather, my mother-in-law and I would like to do this for you."

Imagine that! Never had I experienced such generosity in my life – and from someone who a week earlier had been a complete stranger. After working through the surprising degree of difficulty that I'd experienced in receiving a gift of this magnitude, I knew quite clearly what would happen next. I graciously received the offering, put most of my stuff in storage, and moved to Hawaii to immerse myself in the mystical, shamanic world of Robert Shapiro.

I spent about eighteen months with the focus of the mentorship on Robert's channeling methods, as well as studying and applying the shamanic methods he had been taught throughout his life. I felt incredibly blessed to spend this time learning with him, and as if this wasn't enough, Robert had unknowingly given me another beautiful gift. Between the media projects that I helped him produce, along with a little shopping, cooking, and watching our favorite British mysteries, this beautiful man gave me the space to rest and to remember how to do nothing with no expectations. For the first time in my life, I learned what unconditional love meant – beyond just platitudes and words.

What blossomed from this was finding out and strengthening who I truly was. As a result, another entire body of music arrived, which became CD number three – *Songs of Anima*. Additionally, after months of rest and strengthening my natural way of being, I received the true inspiration and purpose for writing this book – sharing the story of my life with the Visitors, and what I was taught about activating this resonant communion with Love.

I have immense gratitude for Robert Shapiro and Maggie Boyd – two awe-inspiring people, who had never met and lived thousands of miles apart, yet both synchronized to offer a gift to me that forever changed my life. Some would say that I followed my instincts and my heart to connect with these all-important people in my life. I'll go along with that, but it was more. For me, it was the added dimension of the magnetic energy that ignites in my heart, my forehead, the palms of my hands, and the bottoms of my feet.

Since "instinct" and "heart" are words, and overused words at that, I always go with this natural, magnetic dance in consciousness that has never steered me wrong. Robert was the first human being in my life who shared this similar identification, understanding, and application of the magnetic energy. I was so very grateful for our shared appreciation as well as the mirroring of our understandings of the natural world and our natural selves. What a gift he has been — and continues to be — in my life and in the lives of countless people around the world. And I'm happy to say that Maggie and her lovely, generous heart are still a treasured part of my life too. Blessed am I!

IX

The Natural Self
Beyond What We Are Told

---∞---

Dear God, I was wondering
What day you might be coming home
We've missed you
But we're doing the best we can
With what we know
It's everything we've been told...[18]

~ E. MEYER (LYRICS)

I loved Hawaii and her many gifts. Beauty was something that could be seen and felt on a constant basis, and it was highly conducive to the full-immersion study and practice of shamanic, feminine wisdom. I was quite physically active at the time. I had a running and exercise routine that I very much enjoyed. This was new, as I'd never been much of an athletic type before. Guidance was clear that I needed this body health and balance for the ongoing schedule of changes and integration in consciousness.

Robert had a sleep-work routine that was opposite mine, so I found myself living a quiet and solitary life. I know many would not refer to this as heaven, but for me, it most certainly was. I returned to a methodical same-time, same-place practice of the Presence – aka meditation. It was a way of being that had transformed my consciousness before the turn of the century, and it had effected great movement and change in my outer life as well.

Robert taught me the art of verbal channeling, which I applied and practiced daily. I'd already had a life history of contact from beyond the average bandwidth of consciousness, so naturally I began to synthesize and eventually demonstrate my own approach to matching, blending, and translating frequency. I was also honored that Robert shared more with me in the way of resonant tools that he later offered to the public in his book, *Benevolent Magic and Living Prayer.* These tools, as well as other powerful shamanic applications, have been welcomed and integrated into my own healing work today.

Sprinkled throughout my journals from the 1980s to the mid-2000s were dreams, visions, and multidimensional experiences that I had recorded. These were introspective thoughts and inspirations about my life and then random blurbs of automatic writing that followed visitations. I never questioned any of it, and I was unaware at the time that I was in the beginning stages of developing my own verbal translations of energy. However, I hid them away and rarely spoke about them with anyone. Robert was guided that he could not listen to mine, or anyone else's translated material for that matter, so I rarely received any outside validation for what I was recording. Still, the verbal messages poured through, and they always came with profound love and guidance.

I recall feeling that I'd found my ultimate path – to be a channeler. Finally, I'd come to the place where my life would make sense – the place where I would have purpose. I would now channel messages from the space beings!

Nope. That wasn't it – not exactly anyway.

I was continuously disappointed with what came through me. It wasn't because it didn't feel true and profound. It was because I couldn't find anything in the vast channeling world that was like what was coming through me. More importantly, though, when I compared myself to Robert, Darryl, or any other channeler at the time, I was convinced that I must be doing it wrong. What I brought through didn't seem to generate excitement for most people who were drawn to these types of cosmic or ET messages. Perhaps it was because in most cases, the Intelligence that I translated, strongly suggested that humanity shift from "endless seeker" status and empower themselves to fully actualize on Earth.

Still, I continued to record them – evolutionary-themed messages and practices that refused to be connected to existing ET stories and characters or any established infrastructure for explaining the unknown. In fact, I was told repeatedly by these energetic infusions that I was blending or communing with aspects of myself that were far beyond adequate translation to 3D. The focus with my connections was about the evolution of human consciousness and the reactivation of our natural design and capacities – both individually and collectively. None of it would fit nicely into the existing containers of science, religion, New Age, UFOology, and so on. Believe me, this pretty much made me invisible in the world. I had no familiar framing or terminology for the minds of seekers, certainly no entertainment value. Still, it wasn't as if I could easily dismiss it and move on. It was my entire life – a lonely and painful place indeed. Sadly, I had become used to living on the fringe of programmed consciousness. If the visits and associated messages had stopped, believe me, I would have too. It was already too hard to be the "different one" in everyday life, let alone the weirdo on the fringe.

Throughout my interdimensional contact and schooling, I had adapted to a method that was more along the lines of a feeling-decoding translation. I was consistently shown that through the resonant spheres of data that emerged from these fields of energy, I was going "beyond what is known" and returning with pure feeling-knowing. I could only translate for others by harnessing my existing vocabulary and experiential understanding. I liken it to a multidimensional Pictionary game that not only utilizes the description of images but also multiple layers of feelings. Later, the messages began streaming in real time – always with the incredibly powerful magnetic energy holding me in place while I blended with the Intelligence that felt like an epic cosmic family reunion within.

As far back as I can remember, I've always been someone people felt comfortable talking to – from total strangers to friends and coworkers. I found myself hearing and seeing things when these people spoke. When people are being sincere and honest with the feelings they share, I naturally receive data by listening to the sound and tones in their voices. It starts the movie within – generating pictures and feelings that I decode and pass on if this is asked for. Some might call this psychic. But the info I receive has nothing to do with fixing or designing a more comfortable human life in the context of the past (for example, relationship, career, money). It's a bit more transformational than that, which explains the initial unpopularity of it! The guidance is about letting go of all that we were told so that we might locate the truth within and heal this into a blended state of wholeness. What this looks like – both individually and collectively – is something we may have the joy of seeing in this lifetime.

The more clearly the clients speak the truth about what they are feeling (what is actual), the more data I receive from their Souls about their unique paths to integrating more of their Universal Identity in their lives on Earth. If appropriate, I then translate their expanded, or Soul Selve's, messages. Through this blended awareness, guidance emerges to support and assist with the design and tooling of each unique roadmap to wholeness. When people contact me for support, I find that it's usually indicative of what their souls intended for this time of awakening. If I can feel the strong presence of their Greater Selves, this alone is the indicator that I might be able to help them build a bridge to Universal Consciousness.

In the beginning, the data is only provided to ignite or inspire the clients to begin. I then encourage them to build trust in their own attentive practice toward the actualization of their souls on Earth. While some of what I do may end up sounding like what others do, detachment from what has always been and what others are doing, was crucial in my development of these skills. We may inspire each other – always – but ultimately, I am informed, every individual must go direct in meeting, communing, and realigning with our Greater Consciousness and Source. Following this, we develop the communities to support and reinforce each other in our collective practice of wholeness.

I find it far easier to connect with the new children here than I do my own generation. To me they feel like embedded evolvers for humanity. These kids not only arrived with more of their universal awareness and profound abilities intact; they refuse to participate in the collective, cultural lies and inefficient systems adopted by previous generations. They're not interested, nor do they choose to waste energy on enabling anyone – even family members – in covering up the truth. If they do, you can bet they will exhibit imbalances that could surface in distorted, emotional behaviors. This covering up of the truth can be as simple as our words and behavior not matching what we are actually feeling or broadcasting – something that we older generations were taught to accept as *normal.* One of the labels assigned to this obvious rejection of the mechanics of *how things have always been* is the autism spectrum. After reading a book on the subject years ago, I was convinced that I was on the spectrum as well. (See chapter 13 for more about these new children.)

When I am in the presence of these new kids, I have noted that I connect with their hearts rather quickly, and data is exchanged through a field of understanding before there is even a thought of using language. Thankfully, there are older-generation liaisons popping up now who feel passionately about nurturing and supporting these children, helping them to bridge and communicate with the confusing world they were born into. I have recently concluded that in my interactions with these new children, I am now meeting my "angels with skin on." It's a beautiful thing, and I hope to elaborate on this in the future.

Just as the music arrived in colored spheres of data that I translated into melodies and lyrics, I found that my approach to decoding the energy messages was the same. Never was it an experience of them (the nonhuman intelligence) and me. Rather, it was a pure collaboration of consciousness that, for lack of a better description, wanted to be songs, words, or guidance for others and myself. I always had the strong knowing that I was them yet still Eileen, the human girl. As unclear as it all was with worldly definitions, it was always *very* clear with energy.

Trust me, this has never been a rainbows-and-fairies kind of reality. It is only now, sitting on my twenty-first century perch, that I'm able to see the blessing of it all. For most of my life, it was extremely challenging, and it demanded a level of courage that I had to show up with, or quite frankly, it felt as if I would die. This may sound melodramatic, but it's not. It's the reality of what felt like a mandatory program to overcome fear and deep conditioning within my emotional and physical bodies.

I was constantly on the edge, pushing the envelope through high-frequency meetings with the unknown. I would also move through bouts of confusion, anger, and what-the-f#@k meltdown rants. Nothing made sense in the so-called normal world after repeated explosions into wider context. In addition, I had to continue fitting into the world without completely losing my mind. It is only now as I write this body of work that a synthesis of random, seemingly unrelated pieces of my life are becoming far more cohesive in my consciousness, but I still cannot be organized and deliver them in the same old linear ways that most would prefer.

The same themes from the past kept repeating. I still felt alone. I still felt the envy from watching others have enjoyable and successful lives within the bandwidth. And I still felt as if I had been repeatedly plucked from the agreed-on reality in order to adapt to frequencies that could not help but destroy any deference to the existing game. Was that part of the plan? Perhaps. Still, there were times that I begged to be free from the loneliness of the uninterpreted view. It reminds me of the famous scene with Morpheus in the film, *The Matrix*. I petitioned many times for the blue-pill, but I don't recall ever being presented with a choice. Why? Apparently, I had swallowed the red pill long ago.

This is your last chance. After this, there is no turning back. You take the blue pill – the story ends, you wake up in your bed and believe whatever you want to believe. You take the red pill – you stay in Wonderland and I show you how deep the rabbit hole goes.

~ MORPHEUS, THE MATRIX

My rabbit-hole versions of the red pill delivered a lifetime of bioenergetic-lightning episodes in my physical body, massive data dumps, trips through walls and windows that led me to ships and other worlds for teachings, roundtable discussions, surgeries, and dozens of interdimensional pep talks. Most of the communication occurred through a natural or innate mechanism – a heart-based, telepathic communion. On other occasions, I found I was naturally reading and speaking in otherworldly languages, but these languages feel ancient, like remnants of pre-telepathic consciousness.

I have become aware of reports of some of the younger-generation contactees experiencing the languages – in both written and audible form. My advice continues to be: immerse yourself in the resonant love that arrives *with* the associated, outer forms of communication. It is the energy, and the recalling of your connection to it will activate the physical episodes, open the doorways, and deliver far more understanding and remembrance. This occurs in an instantaneous, multidimensional-frequency form that is far superior to the linear decoding of written or verbal languages. In my own experience, the words and sounds are like a key that opens the doorway to these multidimensional worlds – where we easily reconnect with other aspects of our selves, or Source. When I listen back to some of my recordings with these strange sounds – everything from pops and clicking, to breath and tones, to foreign-sounding words – it ignites my entire body and being within seconds, and I'm fully immersed in the resonance of direct knowing.

Over time, I understood and surrendered to the importance of their work – a busy entourage of out-of-focus, odd-looking physicians who delivered a tiny hybridized being from my womb and seemingly performed numerous upgrades on all levels of my hardware and software. Then there was the pure sound and light intelligence. I still don't know whether the messages pour through my mouth from an activation of what is already downloaded and stored in my cells or whether it is streaming in the moment – or both. All of it seemed to enhance my senses over time as well as helped to restore a more whole-heart, whole-brain perspective. With this came more expanded abilities – some I have been actively exercising, some surprise me in the moment when they are needed, and some remain more dormant for a future time.

Flash forward for a moment. I was preparing to give a talk to a small group in Tucson, Arizona, in the early summer of 2015. I felt a bit more nervous than usual, so I knew something was up. It turns out that we went into a full-on demo of how the physical body – ahem, my body – responds and adjusts to the frequencies when it blends with my consciousness. Before this timing, it had always occurred when I was alone. There I was, moaning and sounding and appearing to be having an orgasm – in front of about forty unsuspecting people. The messages began shortly after I returned to a balanced, integrated place. I was well aware of the embarrassment and shame that people were feeling with this, but there's nothing I could do at this point.

In actuality, my body and being naturally moves in the direction of rising and meeting this Love rather than remaining in the space of polite, well-mannered containment. We've come a long way from my healing-school days when I could still actively and persistently suppress it.

I was a child born into the linear norm of America, yet I have memory of naturally perceiving and engaging with life and other life forms in a more spherical way. It's clear to me now that most human beings arrive this way. Soon we are absorbed into the population at the speed of our environmental conditioning – from a natural, infinite ball of connectivity into the more acceptable linear existence. Most people I encounter have very little memory of our more innate, holistic way of perceiving – where innocence and honesty are of the highest order. Some of us still enjoy our fantastical nighttime dreams, oftentimes returning with dream symbols that stand for a more holistic or quantum experience that we were actually having, but it is quickly dismissed. While I believe the majority of us have memories of being more imaginative, loving, and carefree as children, sadly, in order to fall in line with the programming here, these remain distant memories or symbols that are relegated to the fantastical. In other words, it becomes no longer applicable or translatable to our smaller-bandwidth lives.

It seems that we've all adapted to symbols and systems outside ourselves – including language and money – to organize our thoughts, values, and reality here. The more of ourselves is soon pushed away, compartmentalized, or pressed into something distant or unrecognizable. What grows from what we have been given permission to reside in is a small patch of awareness – a confusing, limited, patriarchal orientation to life. This orientation is quite clearly accomplished through established systems of education, religion, politics, and other cultural dictates. It is quite an impressive program indeed, but it need not limit our consciousness.

What happens when we are exposed to more? And by "more," I am referring to a stream of data that arrives via an entirely different network or grid of understanding. It is not symbolic; it is actual. It only becomes symbolic when we attempt to translate it. I can clearly imagine now that when two or more points of individual consciousness become actualized, translation is no longer required. When we generate a field of resonance, words go out the window. Music or poetry may still be a desirable way to speak or sing resonance because it's fun to create, but words can become heavy and laborious (explain drain) once the body and consciousness adapt to resonance communion. This restoration of our natural state is occurring and achievable now.

The year 2005 was a big year for me in the area of translation. I did my best to keep up with all the frequency messages that wanted to be words and assembled into published material one day. I was first aware of a message by a field of energy enveloping me – not unlike the energies I felt when a visit was about to occur. While I constantly doubted my abilities to accurately translate this much data, I did my best. If I spoke something that wasn't quite right, though, my body would let me know. The Intelligence would stop the streaming and I would reorient, retune, and rephrase.

For the most part, I caught on to the method and intent of this group consciousness, and I grew in my proficiency to reduce it to words. Later, the Intelligence taught me how to translate from resonance – generated through an honesty and innocence practice that I will outline in chapter 12. It is a practice of fine-tuning frequency and then meeting and blending with the greater aspects of Self. It always arrives in a multidimensional form, and there's always a feeling of "this is way too much to make into a sentence or paragraph."

After reviewing my own translations, I noted that some translated beautifully. Most times, though, I felt anxious and frustrated, as I was still aware of so much more than what language could accommodate. Sometimes I had to fill in or round out the translated message with all that was hanging in the ethers – images, feelings, and so forth. Other times, more would unexpectedly drop in later to add to the existing text. All these aspects of me were doing our best to honor the inspirational messages. It took many more years to come, to play with it, practice, experiment, and ultimately translate more efficiently. Below are a few excerpts of these earlier translated messages.

Verbal Transmission: June 3, 2005

You will find that what works for you can work for many, many people, for that is the beauty of this work. It is a demonstration of how these changes and these shifts are made within the individual consciousness, which is connected to all of consciousness. And in your particular focus, as we have indicated many times, the demonstration of these principles and these teachings is crucial within your realm – crucial in order to inspire. You will find that words alone will not inspire any longer, for these mental projections, these concepts that are attached to words and phrases, are losing their charge as more and more people revert to heart cognition.

Verbal Transmission: August 24, 2005

In the past, these connections have been more of a reaching through the human dream, the mental projections, with many filters. This is not a judgment of humans. This has been the collective reality. This is what has been set up and defined for this existence. And benevolent beings have reached out and stretched to find their way to your consciousness through the definitions that you have created. When one becomes more integrated – referred to as feminine and masculine balance – you are naturally supported to know communion, interdimensional communion.

This demonstrated will feel and look more like a blending. Those who commune may choose to commune in deeper ways, and they will also notice that the knowings arrive unexpectedly as they have opened to becoming more – to manifesting more of their identity here on Earth.

There is a perception, generally, in the way that channeling has been perceived in the past, based on limited awareness of how the mechanics of consciousness works, for it is not simply mechanics. There is a more holistic view of the channeling process. So there is the stepping-aside perception for another being to come through in the mechanistic thinking. In the holistic and natural approach, it resonates with the natural frequencies and allows the blending to occur. There is translation in this form. Translation occurs without thought. So it is more of the intuitive *body that is assisting in translation. This is where we have flashes of inspirations, revelations, and lightning-speed understandings and knowings, for this is an activation of an ability that is inherent within the natural human. I, and we, are not a separate entity speaking through this human. This human has been activated to reconnect more consciously to the natural world around her not only on her planet but also throughout the universe.*

This energy is not "other." This is the natural self. It is manifest, demonstrable in time. This is the birth that you seek.

Verbal Transmission: November 6, 2005

This transformation, this evolution, is occurring within consciousness – first the understanding that it is possible to make new choices within your own consciousness and then to make those choices. It is not necessary to create so much of the outer-world storms and chaos and disruptions if humans on a rapid, accelerated scale begin to choose to return – "re-turn." This is not going back; it is turning toward the Source Frequency to allow greater and greater understanding of your capacities and to consciously ask and state that this is what you choose: to awaken into wholeness, and conscious, active participation, and responsibility for what is occurring now. There are humans who serve as portals for these re-minding energies, for the changes will not occur with concepts, language, words, or the intellect. The changes will occur in the feeling realm within the feeling body. So continue with your prayers to accept your fullness in this space-time construct.

Thank you for your courage to open in this way and to practice connecting – to be the child once again who has not yet been introduced to the idea of judgment. The child lives within the imaginal realm – the magical realm, the natural realm. Continue with your journey AS that child and you will receive more strength, power, knowing, and ability to demonstrate the natural human in your world.

Now, when you begin to share in this way with other people, they will either resonate with this or they will not. If they find it necessary to go out and compare what you are saying to what others are saying, or to what they believe, it resonates or it does not. It will both feed them and support them, or it will not. It matters not whether it fits into the mentally projected realm. We are not saying that there is nothing of value in the mentally projected realm. There are scattered truths throughout, but it's primarily fragmented. It is the image of a shattered mirror – little pieces, little reflections, but there is not a cohesive connection. This is what you have been living within, and we see you, this being Eileen, sifting through all of the little pieces of reflection, attempting to find the truth that you are feeling in your being, in the piecing together of these little mirrors scattered about. This is understood. And this is a stage of development. But we believe at this time that you have stood up. You have dusted yourself off, and you have withdrawn your interest in finding validation for what you feel and know within the scattered debris of mental projection. You're coming home to the heart, honoring the heart, valuing this way of being in the world, and strengthening yourself, for you have been criticized, and we cannot shield you from further criticism in your life for what you are doing.

X

When the Heart is Ready
The Sacred Stone

—❦—

We will awaken our spirits again. When that happens, things
will be revealed of the old wisdoms. Things that have been
forgotten for a long time are going to be brought back: Art,
Music, Song, Dance, Storytelling, Spiritual Wisdom, knowl-
edge, and the wisdom of how to work with Mother Earth,
will all be restored.[19]

~ LARRY MERCULIEFF
TO THE ALEUT ELDERS IN ALASKA
— PASSING ON THE MESSAGE OF HOPE FROM
THE HOPI, MAORI, AND THE STONY ELDERS

It was the spring equinox, March 20, 2005. I went for a walk just south of Santa Fe, New Mexico, where I was house-sitting for a friend. This was a job-living arrangement that fit well with my ongoing gypsy-like, transitional, learning lifestyle that was occurring between Hawaii and Santa Fe. On this particular walk, I felt balanced and full of gratitude. I was content with my ongoing project to allow a more expanded yet solid worldview manifest in my everyday life, and I was determined to live passionately and authentically. On this day, as is reflected in my journal, I was quite happily hanging out in the moment – having had several demonstrations in recent years that all my needs are met as long as I live presently and ask for what I need. This is not to say that I was always present and never felt fear. Believe you me, it crept in – the fear of starvation, being insane, becoming homeless, or all-of-the-above definitely arose. But with the tools that I had been given through inspiration and serendipitous meetings with both nonphysical and physical friends and allies along the way, I was able to embrace the fears and receive guidance for the next steps and the next. And it was on this day that I encountered one of the greatest pearls of all.

I remember feeling quite content as I stopped to rest and to breathe in the gorgeous Santa Fe breeze. I was near the end of my hike, and because I was alone, I felt and spoke out loud to the trees, thanking them for teaching and demonstrating beauty and grace. Even as a child, I had always noticed that the trees, the plants, the animals, the water, and the rocks – especially the rocks – never had any trouble fully radiating the energetic presence of who they are. I could easily feel it, and it was always nurturing and transformative to me. I was blessed to have this restorative alliance – purely and simply. These present-moment teachers are all around us, infusing us with the memory of what it feels like to be interconnected and whole. It can't help but have a powerful feeling effect on those who pass through their balanced world.

With a full heart, I walked back up the hill toward the house. Quite unexpectedly, I became aware of a magnetic connection that was being made between my right palm and a particular spot on the ground to my right. I noticed that the hotspot in my palm became active. When I use that term "active," what I mean is that the center of my palm lights up with energy. It tingles, and it has a warm and intensely pleasurable energy that travels up my arm and explodes into my heart area. It naturally radiates throughout my body in the very same fashion as the previously described bliss experiences. While I have felt this unusual occurrence to some degree throughout my life, significant upgrades of this energy in my right palm began in 2003, during a particularly powerful vision in which I was shown and informed by the Presence that I carried the "spiral in the giving hand." Of course I wondered about the meaning of this from time to time, especially when it was activated, but I've since given up on analyzing or Googling it to see whether anyone else experiences this phenomenon with the same name. I simply filed it under, "It is what it is."

In this particular moment, it was as if a stream of energy went from my heart and right palm to a collection of stones, or perhaps it was more from the stones toward me. Either way, I was literally captivated by it. I could not have taken a step further because the magnetic connection created a sort of force field that strongly suggested I stay put. I felt no fear; by this time, my body and being were quite familiar with this compelling and extraordinarily loving energy.

I squatted down and began to speak with the stones. I don't remember what I said. The words and sounds just seem to flow out of me. Aboriginal people refer to this experience as the Dreamtime. This word feels good to me, so I use it in my descriptions from time to time. I spoke to the stones, and it became a simultaneous asking and knowing what this powerful connection was about. I felt an invitation to make physical contact, so I reached out to touch one particular stone, an ordinary looking river rock that seemed to "light up" more than the others. From that point on, it is difficult to recall or translate all that had happened. I'm only able to describe it as if I am translating a dream that I had the night before.

It was a magical connection that happened on many levels, and it seemed to go far deeper than other mystical experiences I'd had in the past. It's as if it opened up a portal within me in order to communicate and to better hear and understand the language of the stone. The stone communicated through a natural feeling language with added images in my third eye. It was made clear to me that it did in fact want to come with me. I felt and saw an image in my mind's eye of the stone being placed on my solar plexus and sleeping with it in this position on that very night. In this expanded state, I had no doubt in my mind about what I was seeing and feeling. I knew in deeply profound ways that it would be beneficial to my spiritual growth and understanding, a vital piece in my ongoing request to live more fully, benevolently, and consciously with the natural world. In fact, it felt like a major nod and validation from Gaia that the earlier communion messages were true – our alignment with the planet, our Mother, is vital for our full awakening and further evolution of consciousness, as we are absolutely evolving with her.

I spent most of the day communing with this stone, reaching ecstatic states and revelatory states, and also hearing new music and tonal understandings. The very thing that I had been mulling over in the morning before my walk (and had reached no particular conclusion about) was the topic of divination tools – tools such as astrology and numerology, and other methods for knowing and seeing more. I was feeling upset about a recent reading in my life that left me feeling disempowered. While I was drawn to use these tools in my life from time to time, I decided that I no longer wanted to utilize them if there was negativity, fear, and shame associated with the interpretations. I don't like to feel bad or disempowered when I am receiving or doing a reading for myself, and I would certainly not want to be in a position of contributing to someone else's sense of disempowerment by regurgitating the older, fear-based interpretations of what the symbols mean. I choose to see and experience life as benevolent and empowering now. So how does one utilize divination tools in a completely heart-centered and benevolent way? Is that even possible? Yes.

In holding the stone on that afternoon and being in quite a powerful Dreamtime/altered state, I was given what seemed to be a complete answer to my earlier questions. Now, this comes as a direct result of holding the stone. Never mind that up until this time, in all my naiveté and innocence, I hadn't yet become aware that stones had been used by Native cultures and mystics, in both ancient and recent pasts, to divine or see! A series of synchronistic events led me to this information, and this stone became the prelude to opening to other resonant forms of translation. Just as I was strongly encouraged to do so many years ago, I knew it was important for me to keep record of these happenings. I was never fully clear why, but the loving, magnetic energy always moved me to do so.

There has been a definite evolution in receiving insights from the stone. The stone made it very clear early on that in order to "see" or receive, I must be familiar with the feeling language of the natural world. And the more innocent and truthful I am in this feeling dialogue, the clearer and more revelatory the experience of "knowing" is. The best way to explain what comes through the stone in these communion states is a big sphere of light and resonance that contains everything and more – infinity, actually – of what I am asking about. Now, understand that if I begin to speak about it in real time, then I am stepping out of the center of this bubble, and I begin translating this body of wisdom that has come. And as always, in translation to words, there is room for error, because a lot of what comes in this way is not translatable to language. I don't want to translate when I'm in the knowing sphere. I have found it to be quite hard work to pull myself out of that magnetic bliss.

I translate it, though, because I'm so excited about the information that is coming. Yet at the same time, I am shown that this pure-knowing field is something we all have the ability to shift directly into should we choose. The stone showed me that speaking our feelings out loud – honestly and innocently – will clear, retune, and realign our individual consciousness and bodies with the knowing state when we are feeling off, unbalanced, or afraid.

I am able to understand now that we are not at the mercy of our three-dimensional interpretations of planetary aspects, or divination cards, psychic interpretations by others, or even worldly interpretations from our own cultures and governments, for that matter. I was shown that there is the smaller bandwidth of frequency in which we have moved about, and while we have choices within this existing bandwidth, they have been limited. At this time, we have the ability to transcend the agreed-on bandwidth – if we invite the truth of our natural, feminine, instinctual selves back in to marry and "fill in" the rest of our consciousness. We simply cannot transcend our limited view with only an image or symbol of ourselves – or the view from the language-based intellect alone. It must first be balanced and actual. A new reality is born from the foundation of this whole and present moment.

Verbal Transmission: April 15, 2007

Bring your attention to the present moment, and this attention to the present moment can be done through speaking out loud. Firstly, you may be speaking thoughts out loud, for you are not accustomed or you are deconditioned to speak from feelings. So speaking thoughts, initially, are a way to begin speaking what you are feeling.

Your bodies are connected to Mother Earth. Mother Earth knows and is speaking in actual terms now during her changing and her future changing. She has agreed to provide, shall we say, your sustenance and your backdrop for your experience here for a time. Now you are being called to find your center, your core of Life, your Source, and your passion – which is Life – your own aliveness! Do you know that Mother Earth, at this time and in the coming future times, is choosing Life now? So at this time you may see more and more Earth changes, and you may see more and more loss of life on this planet in the coming times. This is not to be feared, for this is the message from Mother Earth. All that she is doing is shaking off death. She is letting go of all that is life-less on Earth, for she must let go of all the dying and the dead in order to retrieve all of her energy to be fully alive again. And guess what? You are doing this too. You are doing this in your own individual lives. You are doing it collectively with humankind, and you are doing it with Mother Earth. You are doing it with your solar system. You're doing it with your Sun. It is all concurrent. And the choice is Life – conscious aliveness. And your body is your way to full restoration while in form. Your body is your full and equal partner in this, just as Earth is.

So are you alive? Now, being an image or symbol, being an intellectual projection of something that you think you are supposed to be at this time, is not Life. That is a ghost. Ghosts will not survive these transformational changes in the direction of life and balance and harmony with All That Is. So begin right where you are. Begin partnering with your bodies – welcoming and becoming present with the feelings, becoming present with your thoughts, becoming attentive to how you move and operate in your life.

Notice what is happening in your outer world. How are you being informed? Who informs you? Is it the news anchor on TV? Is it your father, your mother, or your teacher? Is it your priest, your rabbi, or your minister? Is it your Bible or your Koran? Is it the Internet? Is it your spiritual guru? You are moving into the stage of your evolution where you must be the authority now. You must accept your own authorship of your life. And do you know who the author is? It is All of Creation living and moving through you in balance and in harmony – healing and restoring. All your misperceptions have occurred because you decided to participate in your own virtual reality.

You decided to create your own game that you project your character into. This character that you call yourself is busy with a job, busy surviving, because this character agrees [with the belief] that there is not enough within this realm. So you are all busy securing your position in this projected world. You use all of your energy to sustain the image and sustain your position. You are having relationships with other images in most cases.

Now Mother Earth is saying that this time of playing video games is over. You must return to the truth now of who you are and sustain yourself directly and actually. And it is very, very simple if *you are willing to be sustained by All That Is rather than within the confines and the limitations of your video game. But you must let go of your images first. Most humans will not let go of their images when these images are working well for them. But in the land of video games, everything is temporary, is it not? One day things are going very, very well. And the next day, they are not going well at all because in this game, there is always an unseen opposite.*

When you invite the conscious remembrance of your connection to All That Is – the unlimited nature of your being – you do not operate in fear. You are no longer informed by your fears and motivated by your fears. You are informed now in your reconnected state; you are informed by Love – Universal Love, not the love that has an opposite. This Love has no opposite. **This love is All in All, and you are connected to that. You always have been.** *So whether you are currently in a state of a happy human life or an unhappy human life, things are now moving and changing due to the larger intentions of Life (which you are intimately connected to) – first and foremost Earth and also your Sun and your Moon. You are connected to the other planets as well, but the Sun and the Moon are more intimately connected to your successful functioning on planet Earth.*

These bodies, these beings, are shifting into gear now for full restoration, for full Life. You may join them now through your conscious intention to live fully – to fully live in conscious connection with All That Is. This naturally creates all the abundance that you require – all the sustenance – without limitation and without harming another being on planet Earth or beyond. And it supports your total joy and fulfillment in what you choose to do in your activities. The key here is to know thyself, as it has been said – not know yourself as concept, image, and belief because someone else said "this" or "that" about who or what you are (which is called conditioning), but to know your Self directly.

You have to want this. One way or another you are all trans-forming. Some will lose their bodies and transform onward to other experiences and other reference points in All of Creation. Some of you have chosen to do this [transform] while remaining in form. And you know who you are. So this message at this time is encouraging you to get to know your bodies a little better. Begin to dialogue with your bodies. Yes, have conversations with them. You might be surprised at the lovely responses you receive. And you may wish to extend conversations to other members of the natural world as well. Talk with a tree until you remember how to commune with a tree. Talk with a stone until you remember how to commune with a stone – or the river waters or a flower or a grasshopper or butterfly, any member of the natural world that you are drawn to and that you feel a connection with. For those of you who feel that you want to move with Mother Earth now and live fully, this work with the natural world will be most helpful and most supportive to you now.

When I say the natural world, it is also working with your bodies – becoming more aware of nutrition and of what your body might be suggesting in the form of exercise. Feel the open-ings. Feel what you are drawn to, and honor that in whatever form of diet or exercise. Understand it is not diet in terms of losing weight. Get over that. Get over that! We are speaking of what you are consuming, what you are putting into your bodies. Is it vibrat-ing with Life, or is it vibrating with death? Simply choose Life! And you will have All of Creation assisting you.

Verbal Transmission: June 29, 2007

The timing for these larger-cycle changes has been in the previous few years of your time (~ 2005) and leading up to your 20-teen calendar years. There will be the breakdowns. Some humans have obviously begun this process a little bit sooner than other humans. You are correct in that there must be the breakdown of the rigid and dense belief systems – the density in which so many humans agree to participate in, swim in, and accept as the pool of life. The pool is not well maintained, and most people ignore this fact because they know nothing else. In fact, it isn't even so much perceived as liquid anymore. It has become thick and viscous, and humans are not aware for the most part that they accept this and call this life.

You and many others are in a position to demonstrate what this clear, refreshing liquid feels like – how the human body responds to it and begins its transformative process initiated in the physical first. So it is a bit of gardening that you and others are doing, to reach in and touch that seed at just the right time in their lives, to show them that the seed is there and to awaken the memory of this seed. Now, once that awareness is present, of that seed, it is as you say – when your seed was touched, you could not return to the full acceptance of moving about or trudging about in this stifling pool because you were made aware of the truth of what Life is, what Life feels like.

Once the physical body is touched and awakened from its monotonous, robotic movements in life, the body will not let the human forget. There is a celebration in the body, and as you have described it in the past, it is as if every cell is touched – awakened – and you feel alive once again. The body cannot return to its sleeping state. Once it is introduced to its natural frequency, its natural vibration, it will naturally move in the direction of balance. This movement into the direction of balance begins to restore and heal and align the emotions and the mind, for it is a way for Spirit to enter in through the back door, so to speak, and to ignite this transformational movement from within the density.

You, as humans, have misidentified the physical body with the drudgery. When touched by Spirit, the body will reveal to you that it is in actuality a very spiritual tool, and it has a very spiritual function on Earth – something that will surprise many of you. You have had your conditioning for centuries now – that the body and life on planet Earth is some sort of punishment and that you are, or have been referred to as, a sinner. You are condemned, it seems, until you are released from the prison. And only then can you soar above, high in the heavens, and the angels join you as you celebrate life.

We do not wish to burst anyone's bubble at this point, but that is a fantasy. That is not going to happen. Forgive us for being so bold in that statement, but we are in a position to make such statements because we are of the vibration that you refer to as angels. We are happy to be recognized by humans that we do exist, but you've gotten the story all wrong.

We do maintain the frequency and balance of Love, Peace, and Truth, for that is our natural state. It is your natural state as well. Certainly, we could say that we have been employed to oversee your growth, your evolution as you entered into time and as you will transcend. We are here now because we are fast closing in on that transcending time.

The point here is we want to encourage humans to begin to recognize, to appreciate, and acknowledge this fantastic tool of the physical body. It is a beautiful thing, and it has consciousness and wisdom in and of itself. The tool works best when your consciousness is aligned with it on Earth.

So let us return to that crying-out time – those times when you, as you say, fall, and you cannot seem to get up and make it work anymore. Now, this may come in many forms. It could come through illness or accident; it could also come through simply recognizing that life as you have been taught that it is does not work. I'm sure many of you will agree [that it is not working] by looking at your world stage and the dramas that are taking place in war, poverty, and hunger.

You have participated in creating this world. You cannot disconnect yourself from what you have created. You cannot say, "That is not my fault. It is the president's fault." You have participated and added energy to this collective world. There is the shrugging of shoulders, "Oh well, what can I do? I am only one person." You can do everything – everything. By choosing to break the addiction to serving things as they have always been, agreeing to all that is known and all that has been. Break that addiction now, stand in the center of the present moment, and proclaim that you are here now. And ask. Ask for healing in your own misperceptions about life and your own sense of self. Ask for this balance. Ask to be shown where your power lies. Ask to be shown what you can do to help shift the world, to restore the world to its natural state.

Do not be surprised after this powerful present-moment conversation that things begin to change in your life. You will be taken to those places within yourself where you are starving, where you are in poverty, and where you are warring within yourself. This is powerful work. It is conscious work.

You do not need to do the work if you are not inspired to be whole. There is an opportunity here in these coming years to heal and to give birth to wholeness on Earth. That is all. If you choose to deliver your consciousness to wholeness in another way, that is up to you and your greater Self as to what path and what direction you move. We are simply here to assist you in remembering the overall plan.

These are marvelous times. Most certainly there is evidence of pain and suffering on your planet, and you are in charge of changing that. No pressure! It's just an opportunity. You are not alone. Never have you been alone. Gold-Light Beings are very much in your midst, working with you, supporting you, and encouraging you to be who you are, to re-turn to that Source frequency – that frequency that you have projected on to what you call God or angels. That is your core frequency as well.

Humans have labeled the compartments of consciousness; truly there are no compartments of consciousness. There is what you choose to see and what you choose not to see. The energy, the passion – the love – is beginning to flow into human con-sciousness. This liquid love is moving in because enough humans have been welcoming it. Therefore, it will begin to move your vis-cous, cluttered pool that you have claimed as "life," and you will begin to feel the movement.

This is nothing to fear, but you may feel fear because you are used to staying stuck or moving very little. Allow the move-ment. Allow and witness in the present moment, your fears. Feel the pain in the present moment. Stay in that vibrant spotlight of present, and this liquid love will pour in and show you who you are beyond a shadow of a doubt. We are not saying "show you" in concept. We are saying it will show you in your body what Life is.

For some, it will take time to adapt to Life in its true state, and that is all right. You take your time. But also notice where you resist Life and Love in universal terms, for it is the univer-sal flow that is moving into your human play, your human con-sciousness, to bring you back into awareness of your true state of being.

Now, we know how much you love to sit around, have coffee, and chat about conceptual things. In these times, there will not be so much of the sitting around to discuss the deeper mean-ings of things or even to gossip about who's doing what and how they're moving through these times. You will be called to experience it, and there will be little "time" to discuss it. Do you see?

The embodiment of Love – the activation of Love within the physical body – will require all of your present-moment attention. Do not be afraid, for you are now in a position to become experts in the transformation of consciousness, and perhaps you shall be employed to oversee or to assist in the evolution of consciousness in other points of reference throughout the universe. The possibilities are endless.

So when the movement begins in your world, in your life, remember in that moment when you feel there is chaos and there is panic and there is crisis, bring yourself to the awareness, the remembrance that – ah! – this is that place of present moment, where I can now ask for this energy to fill me, guide me, and show me a greater way to live. I can ask this loving energy to show me the endless possibilities for Life. We celebrate you, and we cheer you on. Never forget how powerful you are. You are doing magnificent things – every one of you on planet Earth, simply for being in form on Earth at this time. You are celebrated throughout the Universe.

Verbal Transmission: December 26, 2007

Now, there is a message that has come for you this morning, and you began to speak the message. It is the Mother. It is the Feminine, but understand that She is resonant frequency. She is not to be viewed as a human being or as a god or goddess in human form. She may appear this way but only in humans who have accepted the rest of themselves, their wholeness. Then She is present. Any human who chooses to be real at this time – to be honest, to be actual – will feel her presence, and may not name *it Goddess or Divine Feminine. You may name it something else. The point being that you are attached to names and labels and definitions here because your consciousness is framed within language. There are limitations here if you are framing your reality solely within language.*

Some of you feel and receive information through your knowing and feeling capacities, and it is something that feels somewhat foreign to you or unsupported in your reality. If you feel unsupported, you will avoid that which you cannot explain in language. It is as simple as that. You will not give it the attention or the welcoming that it deserves.

Your total understanding comes primarily through this avenue of feeling and knowing. So when you limit yourself to thought and to the intellect to organize and define you, you are fragmenting your consciousness, and you will not feel the fullness that you are capable of feeling as a human being on Earth. It is as simple as that. So welcome and reactivate these feelings that have been judged in your past – ridiculed and criticized and condemned. These capacities are re-emerging within individual consciousness as the Divine Feminine and the presence of the Goddess frequency on Earth now. It will feel new to humans, but it is not new.

It isn't that the Goddess is returning to save humanity. No one is coming to save humanity. But there is guidance. There is love – support – for the transformation that is occurring in your world now.

Identity is at risk. Identity as you have known it and have known yourselves. Losing your identity now will serve you in greater and greater ways. Keeping up with the maintenance of what you have already created as your self, the definition of who you are, and the energy that goes into maintaining that image, drains you now more than ever. You cannot do this any longer. We speak to the translator directly and to any others who may feel that this wisdom is for them at this time as well.

We always – even when this human has a very personal question – respond on an individual and collective level, for you are all connected. You are all moving through this change at this time as the cycles change. The cycles of creation are chang-ing. You will all be experiencing symptoms of this, and you will describe them sometimes similarly, as another human being would, and sometimes in a very different way. It is all right. You do not have to have matching descriptions of your symptoms. It is more important that you speak of your symptoms, though, that you say them out loud and make them real. It is all about being real now, for when you are being real, when you are speak-ing about what is actually happening honestly, deeply (from the core, from the deepest core of your Self that you can find), then you are healing. You are transforming. You are accelerating your transformation.

It will be much easier – these changes – if you are conscious than if you choose to keep these parts of yourself hidden, the parts that resonate in fear. If you wish to keep them hidden, then these times may – may – now, we do not want to make absolute statements about individual experience, but we are saying it may be more painful the more that you hide your fear. You will feel the pressure, the pressure of Love, on the other side and the pressure of the Light pushing. It will tap at first to give you notice that it is cleansing. It is cleansing Earth. It is cleansing you. It is all one.

So at this time, it is recommended that you begin a practice – to those who have no practice or who have been maintaining a spiri-tual framework or an identity from the past. It is recommended that you begin to speak every day. Do not call it meditation. Do not call it prayer. Do not call it any names from the past. Make up a new word. The translator has chosen the word "connecting." "I am going to go in my room now and connect." Make up your own word. You may use the word "connect" if that resonates with you, but practice using new words, for you are reframing your lives and taking responsibility for your own process, your own evolution. So why not pick your own word? It is not up to a guru to tell you the word. It is not up to your religion to give you the word. You make up your own word. You take responsibility now.

Your religions will not save you or help you in these coming times, unless you are connecting directly with your Creator, with Creation. There will be no room for the framing of heroes or mes-siahs or anyone you are projecting on outside yourself that you were told would save you. You must find this – the Christ, the Buddha, Mohammad, the angels, God – within yourselves now. You must find your own hero, your own messiah, in your universal identity.

More than likely, the first word that pops into your mind would be blasphemy. You have been taught that you are not That. You are not God; you are separate from all that is grand, loving, beautiful, and graceful. You are taught that you are sin-ners. I am speaking to those who have adapted the model of Christianity, of Christ on the cross – the story, the hero. These are images. These are stories that have been placeholders for aspects of your consciousness. This is what is ending – your abil-ity to project your fear, your pain, and your suffering, as well as your hope, on to angelic figures, your heroes of the light, your god outside of yourselves. And that is where the stories take place – outside of you.

You are told a story, and you are told what is real and what is not real. You will not have the ability to project any longer in these times. For some, it is coming quite soon, and for others it will be a bit delayed. It depends on your own choices.

You must know your own story. You must own your own story and all your characters. You must observe and you must be aware of this until you fully accept That Which You Are. We do not speak a great deal about what life looks like after you have made this shift into wholeness, understanding, and accepting that you are God in form. You are connected to Source 100 percent. What does life look like? You will find out!

Do you know that some people on your planet are finding out right now what it is like to be God in form on Earth? They are not seen, necessarily. They are not perceived. They are invisible forms of life. Even though they might also be human, they are not necessarily seen, for there is not enough acceptance in the collective sense of humanity of your own wholeness. You see, you can talk all you want about concepts and ideas of wholeness, and that will not create the event. In fact, it will distance you from the actual event when you are trapped in your words and language. If you are open to the feeling of God, the feeling of Source, and to inviting that in in a conscious way, then you will find yourself rapidly accelerating into wholeness.

Are you ready for this? Are you ready to experience Pure Joy, Pure Love, Pure Grace, and Beauty? It is you! All of Creation that you name as beautiful includes you! You will be <u>One with That</u> when you accept it. It is not that you will not use words anymore. You may use words. But understand that you do not live inside the words. There is a larger way of being on this planet. You may choose to use words, and you may choose not to use words. Yet you will all understand each other when you are resonating within wholeness. You will find other ways to communicate, and it will be a joy to discover these things.

There are many ways to meet your maker, and we have discussed this in the past. There are many ways to say yes to Source. Your greatest prison, as we see it, is inside the walls of words and phrases and ideas. What happens when a prison's walls dissolve? What happens to all the so-called sinners resting within the cells, behind the bars of that institution? What happens when one who has been imprisoned is given sudden freedom? Well, some will not see that the walls have dissolved, and they might create the bars and the walls in their minds and stay, for they simply cannot believe that they are free. Well, this is where you all are – right now. Your walls have dissolved, and you do not know it. Some of you are still waiting and praying for those walls to dissolve. Understand that you have designed your own walls and bars now to help you feel safe within what you know.

Know that as we speak to you now, through this being, from our view, you are huddled together in your groupings where you feel comfortable, where you feel community, and where your ideas and concepts are reinforced. You do this for each other. So you are in your cells, in your rooms, huddled together, believing that you are trapped and that you are praying to some outside god to come and release you, to save you. You are already free! Get up and stretch. Walk outside of your prison walls. Walk through the bars. Go and touch a tree. Talk to an insect. Greet the rest of the natural world, the balanced world. Work with the beings in the natural world to redefine yourselves as a whole being. They will assist you.

So what we are seeing in these coming years is that more and more of you will suddenly realize that there actually are no walls and bars any longer. And you will begin to walk on the True Earth. You will walk in the natural world, and you will rediscover your natural state. This is nothing to fear. You are in fear when you stay in your make-believe cells, behind your make-believe bars. That is fear. You are not small, and you cannot convince yourselves any longer that you are small. This is the change of cycles! You are no longer supported in being small, for this time is over. That is all!

So stand up. Do not huddle in the corner anymore. Stand up! Stand tall! Be proud of All that you Are. You have been given these gifts. Many of you are not accepting the gifts. All that is required of you is to say out loud, "I accept the gift of Life now. I want to live. I want to stand tall. I want to walk on Earth feeling my oneness and my balance and harmony with All That Is. And I want to discover what life is like in that state, for this is my natural state, and I accept it." It is very, very simple – very simple.

You are the one who makes it complicated – framed in your languages and your institutions that you and your ancestors decided was the safest way to be to be in order to be protected, to protect you from the outside world that is "dangerous."

You have been informed that the outside world, the natural world – all that is natural, all that is instinctual – is dangerous and bad for you. Your ancestors have passed this down. Now you have the gift of choice. Do you choose to continue to believe that all that is natural, loving, graceful, and beautiful is frightening? It is not frightening. What is frightening is that you choose to stay huddled there – cold and hungry, disconnected from all that you are. You can change it now. Change it. It is up to you.

It is not up to someone outside you. It is not up to your great gurus and teachers. It is not up to some returning messiah-like being to come and to say, "I now heal you. You may stand up and walk." That messiah is in you, and this is what your being, Yeshua came to deliver to you over 2,000 years ago.

There was a man who walked the earth who was named Yeshua, who delivered this message to you that we are delivering now. It is the same message. You are already healed. You are already forgiven. You are already whole. When will you accept this? This is the question. Allow yourselves to be flooded with love.

This will nurture you. It will support you. It will guide you. You will know all that you need to know when you need to know it, when you accept this love-that-informs into your life – and not in terms of what you know or what you think! That is rooted in the past in the way that you have always done things.

There is an entire, holistic reality outside of the framework of your language and all that you know. And you must begin to step into this to experience life in its fullness on Earth. If you do not choose it at this time, that is all right. There is, as we have said, no judgment whatsoever. We are here to inspire those who have come here to remember this while in form, and you know who you are. You know.

When we speak, something happens within you. Something is triggered deep down inside. You feel the truth of what we are saying. You may not know how to proceed or how to be a new human at this time. Do not frustrate yourselves. You do not have to know what it looks like. You simply need to say, "Yes, I choose this, and I know that I have all the help that I need."

You can simply begin to watch and observe yourself. Get up in your cell and begin to move, and practice walking through the bars. What does that feel like? Maybe you say, "Ooh! They are too solid. I cannot go through." Then you may sit back down and speak with feeling, "I ask the Source of All of Creation to help me walk through these bars and to stand tall and to receive the sustenance that is mine simply by being."

You are learning how. You are relearning, and allowing your true nature to come to the surface, to bubble up through, and to be given permission to be here and to walk on this lovely planet Earth. Do you know that all prisoners will begin to support each other? Some will walk through the bars right away and then turn back around and squeal with delight. They will share how wonderful it feels in the best way that they can – in words or perhaps they will simply radiate that joy so that all those who remain in the cell can feel it and will know instantaneously, without words, "Oh! It is possible. It is true. I shall get up and walk through those bars now as well!" And for all those who have walked through the bars and walls, you will celebrate, and you will build community. You will rediscover life in its fullest – healing the past as well as the future, for you will be re-creating yourself from a place of wholeness.

You get to be the ones to discover what that is like, and you will inform us of what that is like, do you see? We want to know! What is that like? We are not in form. We are light. We are energy. We are love – emissaries of love – to remind you, to tap you on the shoulder and say, "You are whole. You are no longer in prison. You may get up and move now!" And what you will gift to us is the wisdom of what it is like to be love in form – in physical bodies on planet Earth. What is that like? We await your report! We await your messages, for they will uplift and inspire many throughout your universe, what you have discovered in stepping into your own freedom and fullness. We thank you for trusting and for taking that first step.

At this point, the message is directed back to me and my point of view:

Now, you may use that message in whatever form you are inspired. What is it like to allow the fullness, the greater identity, on Earth? What is that like? You are discovering this. The messages that you receive, we notice sometimes there is a twinge of fright within you and a hesitancy to accept this greater identity. We are simply saying be aware of how you limit yourself by reduction, by returning to the cell and entertaining those within. [Here they are referring to my avoidance and fear of speaking more about my process and what the songs are about when I perform.] It is enabling, do you see? It isn't about being comfortable in the prison cell any longer. And this is the leap that you are personally taking.

It is time to release all the prisoners. It does not serve any longer to comfort and enable those who choose to limit themselves. All are given the opportunity to walk through the walls in this timing.

This greater identity requires all of your consciousness. You have chosen to walk outside the walls to experience the joy of that and to turn back in the direction of those who remain huddled in their imaginary cells to announce the good news, to radiate that vibration to those who are willing to feel it, and to remember. It is not to walk all the way back to the cell and spend time sitting on the stool and entertaining yourself and the prisoners [singing in bars]. Perhaps you have done that for a time, but don't you see that you, in actuality, cannot be whole when you reserve part of yourself to blend into and remain in the cell?

This message has more feeling than there is linear meaning in the words themselves. The words are only symbolic for what we are truly saying to you. It is in the full acceptance of your greater identity on Earth that you will proceed in abundance and joy. Therefore, follow your feelings. You will know. And you know what is the right movement for you now and what is not. Keep it simple in that way. Do not judge ahead of time. Make a choice. Follow through. Make changes when you feel. You are making this up as you go. There is no schedule, as we have said, and there is no agenda. You are creating this – the blending of you and your greater Identity. And that is what we have to say for now.

You may use what has come previously in this message to share with others. Send it out in whatever form you are inspired. You do not need to concern yourself about your sanity or timing any longer. You are guided. You are guided by All That Is. You are guided by your greater Identity. Love to you.

The feminine
has slower rhythms
meanders,
moves in spirals,
turns back on herself,
finds what is meaningful to her,
and plays.
This is your body,
your greatest gift,
pregnant with wisdom you
do not hear,
grief you thought was forgotten,
and joy you have never known.[20]

~ DR. MARION WOODMAN

XI

Remembering the Universal Language
Transcending Paradox – Honestly

—∞∞∞—

Everybody wants to get enlightened but nobody wants to change. This is the simple, daunting truth that has been staring back at me from the eyes of countless seekers over the years. "I really want to get enlightened," they insist. "But are YOU ready to CHANGE now?" I ask. "What?" is the inevitable response – surprised and even slightly stunned. And I repeat, "Are YOU ready to CHANGE now?" What follows is always a strange and surreal moment of ambiguity, confusion, and backpedaling."
But I thought you wanted to get enlightened…?

~ AUTHOR, ANDREW COHEN

"Speak honestly and the state of innocence is born. Honesty and innocence activates magnetic resonance and harmonic balance with All of Creation."

~ WISDOM FROM STONE,
JOURNAL ENTRY 7/25/06

W hat are you feeling?"
One day, after a few days' stretch of feeling stuck and blue, I sat down for my meditative-connecting time. I had returned to Hawaii a few weeks prior, with stone in hand. On this particular morning, I knew that Robert would be deep into his daytime-sleep shift so I held the wisdom stone in my right palm and began muttering aloud. I was exhausted from feeling alone and confused with my lifetime of huge, untranslatable experiences. I wondered what was expected of me in the world, and I felt afraid of a future point where I would have to leave the only foundation of unconditional support and community that I had found with Robert's mentorship. How was it even possible to continue existing within this interminable paradox? I believe that my biggest fear was that one day I would not only have to fully accept this as real but also expose it to the world. It was just too much.

"What are you feeling?"

The first time I heard this question it was easy enough to ignore. The second time was so forceful that it brought me to a dead stop. I sat for a few moments, sniffling and uncertain that I would even have the resolve to engage – considering that when I do, I expand further, and I seem to create even more distance between me and my family and friends in the outer world. Do I continue to build the courage and trust for this Love to further guide and support me, even though I have no idea where it's going? Is there a plan? Is my role to be a singer-songwriter and hope to one day be relevant enough to sustain myself in the world? Just as a young woman might feel after investing years of time and energy in a relationship: Where is this going? I want a commitment. I want the offspring of our union. If nothing substantial is going to pan out here, I need to move on. Otherwise, what is the point? Who was I kidding, though? I was so far from normal now that I would never find my way back. I felt I could never un-know what I had experienced in actuality and within my physicality. Dear god in heaven.

The presence interrupted my runaway thoughts and stated matter-of-factly,

"In fact it was all of humanity that would forget, or 'un-know,' the truth about who they are."

I was so engaged with the magnetic force of this presence that I couldn't move. Was this coming from the Stone? It sat in my right palm vibrating with so much heart energy and pure pleasure. As consumed as I was, I recall a random thought that I should press the record button, but then again, one-half of this conversation was an inner, un-recordable voice. Later, when the communion was complete, I wrote it all down, easily and effortlessly.

"You talked yourself into it. You can talk yourself out of it."

"I talked myself into un-knowing?" I felt an affirmative "yes" followed by pictures of lots of words.

"Through language – where all-that-is-known-from-the-past is captured and contained within ideas and concepts – symbols, as you say."

I muttered to myself, "So we're doomed, trapped forever in this un-knowing place, because we speak in languages and symbols?"

"You talked yourself into it. You can talk yourself out of it."

I sighed, "Yes, yes, so you said." And then there was a long silence while I felt the magnetic energy increase.

"What are you feeling... honestly?"

"Uh... I feel good?" I said, as if I were a young schoolgirl waiting for the teacher to reward me for my perfect answer.

All was quiet.

I then had a felt understanding that I wasn't really being honest. "Okay," I said, "I feel worried about what's happening to me... like it's getting to be too late to correct my life and go back to what others call 'the real world.' My family thinks I'm being irresponsible... I really don't feel good about our government... the military industrial complex... it's all so glaringly obvious, but people can't see... so frustrating... and you know, the Supreme Court recently..."

I was strongly interrupted by a force of energy within, "Own *your* feelings." This reverberated through every corridor of my being. "Eliminate people, places, and things. You don't need to know why you feel the way you do. Just say what you are feeling, and define the associated body sensations in every moment. State out loud that you are aware that you are feeling something. There are no wrong answers. There are no right answers. There is no praise nor punishment here; only a full, unconditional welcoming of all that you are feeling now. You talked yourself out of Love. This is a way that you can talk yourself back into it."

I was given a few moments to process what I had just heard, or received, through knowing. It came again.

"So, what are you feeling?"

"Oh! ...Um, okay. I already said I felt good... I'm okay, really... [long pause]. I already talk out loud to myself, probably way too much... So, what do you want me to say?"

"Ah, a very telling response."

I sighed. Here we go again. I began to feel a growing irritation. There seemed to be no end to the demands on me for trust – from both worlds, both directions. In one direction, I had to trust that the pure ecstasy episodes were leading to total freedom, and in the other direction, I needed to trust that I could continue to survive within the painfully small world. It seemed all of the risk was on my end.

My sarcastic fatigue started coming through, "Maybe for a change *you* could just tell me what I'm feeling. Maybe *you* can be the translator this time. Please do. You have my permission to translate my squished-in, tiny-little 3D self."

"I *am* you. But more accurately, I Am."

"Oh, well that's great... for you. You get to be All in All and Eternal and Loving and Grand and Spiritual while I'm..."

"It's clear that you've been conditioned to perceive yourself as something other than 'I Am' in this reality. It's a misperception. In thought, it may seem impossible, but there is, in actuality, nothing to overcome. The illusion of polarity can be resolved through feeling and knowing the truth – through frequency."

"Ha! Sounds easy peasy!" My sarcasm wasn't easily contained.

"Yes, the perceived gap is understood. Now, let's fully immerse our Self into that gap. Let's really swim around in it and find out what's here."

Stone in my right palm began boosting the energy. My whole body was vibrating, and my eyes began to water and stream down my face.

"What are you feeling now?"

"Wha? Well... I'm aware that I *was* feeling annoyed..."

"Good. Yes, that moment is gone. What are you feeling now?"

"Th... th... this feeling... is amazing. It's Peace. Freedom... But wait!" I stopped the escalating bliss, "Wait. Is this real?"

"How does *unreal* feel? Do you know? How does *real* feel?"

"Yes, yes! I do know what unreal feels like. It's the bane of my existence! Everybody here thinks that unreal is real. It's completely upside-down! It's insanity! Even this... what is this conversation? It's the most real thing I've ever felt as a human on Earth. And that makes *me* the crazy one here!"

I stood up suddenly and barely caught the stone that almost slipped out of my hand to the floor. I began to cry. Years of being kept in the dark, never fully knowing what this was all about, began to erupt into conscious feeling. The raw pain of being different came ripping through my skin, "Do you want to know what I feel? I feel afraid of losing my mind! I feel alone, helpless, deranged! I'm having a dialog with voices – not just in my head, but in my hands, my whole body! This stone... it shows me... it teaches me a completely different kind of language... that I know and love, yet when I emerge from it and I'm back in the polarity... I don't fully understand my purpose in the polarity. I feel I'll never be able to explain this to other humans. I mean, how is a stone doing this? How do I just see and know? Shit. Shit. Shit! Holy shit this is hard!"

I paused my tantrum for a moment and noticed that I was sinking into another layer of honesty. "I mean... I love this feeling. I want to share it, but the pain of not making a connection to other humans... I feel afraid. I love this dance... living from this place. Still, I just seem to get further away from other people. I don't want to be further away.

I see the examples of our enlightened masters – men usually – being placed on pedestals, worshipped, and every need is taken care of. Their "enlightenment" seems to create a new special job for them in a beautiful castle far away – yet another archetype for us to bow to, here in the tiny bandwidth. I have discovered the feeling key that transcends the bandwidth, the paradox – in actual experience. I want everyone to feel this and snap out of the spell... This is what I want. Hear me now. I need for this and my life... all people to remember what is natural, what is real, and to claim it NOW! My greatest fear is that I will die with this painful awareness of my interconnectivity with All, contrasted with the extremes of being perceived as a crazy, irrelevant, misunderstood, white-bred American woman. I'm not afraid of death. I'm afraid of living out an entire life and failing to help people feel and remember who they are. I'm terrified that I may be failing in my responsibility to this *too-huge-to-explain* Love."

I sat back down – crying from the gut, my eyes, and my nose. It was all pouring through me at once. I hit pay dirt with a very real pain that had managed to surface through the bullshit, but I quickly composed myself, just as I always did when I had lost control. I was crude and unedited, and the air was thick with anticipation as I waited for admonishment. After all, I had misbehaved for feeling rage, for cursing at this angelic and epic-loving energy. In my family life, I had always been immediately punished for expressing anger. In fact, another repetitive phenomenon that I recalled when I would feel deeply, and outwardly question the reality I found myself within, was that I would always be "put in my place" by my policing family and community for feeling anything other than gratitude for what I have. "Hush up. You're fortunate to be healthy and alive. There are children starving in..." But this time, the closing down of my feelings didn't happen. Instead, I felt a very pleasant, refreshing, and encouraging response,

"Not bad. Actually, none of this is bad at all. Let's continue. What are you feeling now?"

At this point, all I remember is that I let loose with a torrent of more feelings. The dam had been breached. After all, I had been given permission, right? This was different. It was a feeling I had never had – full permission to express what I was really feeling, rather than protecting those in my midst from feeling discomfort... from feeling and triggering their feelings... searching for and regurgitating the approved scripts out of fear. Fear of what? Fear of not belonging. Fear of not being loved. Fear of being different. Fear of being purposeless. Fear of being broke. Fear of being invisible. Fear of banishment. Fear of homelessness. Fear of being crazy... I could go on. And I have... in many, many sittings.

The intimacy that I experience with this Presence is mind-blowing – literally. It shows me what Love really is. It fills my entire body and ignites every cell. It holds me. It bridges me into IT. It's ecstasy. It's enlightenment. I begin to embody it and practice it in the world. I continue to strengthen it in each lucid sitting. I find that even though I am still in the world and confronted with the agreed-on program, along with the associated dialog, every single day I'm learning how to remain aware of energy and navigate. I am witnessing everything – including the knee-jerk responses that we offer up unconsciously in our everyday lives, like...

Joe: "Hi, Eileen. How are you doing?"
Me: "Good, thanks. How are you, Joe? Nice weather we're having."
Joe: "Indeed. How's the job going? Good thing the weekend's almost here."
Me: [in my head]: *Ah, F*@k. Not again. Do I enter this world of repetitive scripts and speak this language? Sigh. How can I expend the least amount of energy in this moment?*
Me: [out loud]: "Yeah Joe, thank god for the weekends. Gotta run. Have a great day!"

Through my lucidity today, I see that whether it is an everyday, mundane conversation or what we deem to be the greatest intimacy a human can experience – sex – we are still cleverly programmed to be allegiant to our worldly markers of money, class, and power within the smaller bandwidth, along with the approved superficial scripts. For most of my life, communication has been painful – simply because I felt that very few people were actually making a connection – communicating something original and authentic. Incidentally, I used to go along with the idea that sex was the greatest feeling ever but not anymore. I have felt a "currency" within that far outshines routine human orgasms, or a large bank account of symbolic currency, for that matter. True intimacy is vulnerability, a full willingness to feel and embody our full value, and share honestly and joyfully with one another. Personally, I haven't known many people in my life who have the courage to expose themselves beyond the safety of their conditioned identities and related needs. Most of what I sense beneath the surface of others is a deep sadness and a constant seeking of relief or distraction from feeling the secret traumas that lie beneath the linear script and stage. I've noticed that if life requires *actually* feeling something, and going off-script to discover the deeper deposits of truth and value inside, we can literally watch *The Matrix* glitches occur in others' eyes. "No!" it says. "Never! This does not compute. Dismissed! Goodbye!"

> *Underneath everything in your life, there's that thing, that*
> *forever empty. Do you know what I'm talking about? Just*
> *that knowledge that it's all for nothing, and it's down there.*
> *Sometimes when things clear away, you're in your car, and*
> *you start going, "Oh no, here it comes," …the [feeling] that*
> *I'm alone. It starts to visit on you… just this sadness.*
> *Life is tremendously sad, just by being in it.*
> *And so you're driving and then [feeling it coming up] you go,*
> *"Ah, ah, ah…" That's why we text and drive. I look around.*
> *Pretty much 100 percent of the people driving are texting.*
> *But people are willing to risk taking a life and ruining their*
> *own because they don't want to be alone for a second. I start-*
> *ed to get that sad feeling. I was reaching for the phone, and I*

said, you know what? Don't. Just be sad. Just let the sadness
hit you like a truck. And I let it come, and I started to feel,
oh my God! And I pulled over, and I just cried. I cried so
much… and it was beautiful. Sadness is poetic. You're lucky
to live sad moments. And then I had happy feelings. Because
when you let yourself feel sad, your body has like, antibodies.
It has happiness that comes rushing in to meet the sadness.
So I was grateful to feel sad, and then I met it with true
profound happiness. It was such a trip.
The thing is, because we don't want that first bit of sad, we
push it away with a little phone… or for the food, and you
never feel completely sad or completely happy. You just feel
kind of satisfied with your products, and then you die.[21]

~ LOUIS C.K., CONAN SHOW

As a child, I hated lying about my feelings, but it's clearly the modern-culture MO here from day one. Never reveal what you're actually feeling. It upsets people. It upsets the status quo. It upsets the program. Because I have had the bioenergetic-based, transformative experiences, the cells in my body have recalled what universal connection feels like. I have this physical marker now. Therefore, it is nearly impossible at this point to defer to the status quo. I am unable to comply with the existing outer story of normal – in the form of relationships, work, religion, politics, and so on. The motivation now is to be present and aware – long enough to create an authentic life, and to cocreate the same in conscious community with others.

Through these honesty and innocence exercises, I learned that never revealing actual feelings leads to never being actual, or fully realized, beings on Earth. We agree to be a symbol or identity in this matrix – an identity that works *for* the matrix – literally. And we all seem to enable each other to remain in this limited place. If you are still a natural child or one of the new humans who has refused to bury your sight and empathy, you may notice that people's outer behavior and identities don't usually match the frequency of what they broadcast. It must be why humans are so terrifying to other beings in the natural world and why benevolent beings from other dimensions won't make overt contact with us – yet. It makes perfect sense to me.

Even the seemingly *nice* humans with nice outer behavior cannot get past the empathic radar of the conscious ones, as they have not un-known their instincts. These awake humans can easily sense the vibe of discord and dishonesty that seeps out from the reservoir of unconscious feelings in others. They know that this, and deeper unconscious trau-mas, can be triggered, and at any moment could emerge violently and unpredictably – sometimes even surprising the *nice* ones themselves. It's not a judgment. Most of us simply forgot and easily suppressed the truth of who we are simply because our conditioning has not given us permission to be authentic.

Verbal Transmission: April 4, 2010

The humans who have had the experience, the exposure to Universal Love, benefit greatly from the memory of it within the physical body. It is not memory in the same way that you identify with the mind or the brain. Memory within the body is knowing information; you have been informed by Love, if you will, and it is there in the cells of your body. Therefore, when you become conscious enough to ask or recall the experience of love on a regular basis with the intention of re-identification with Love, the physical body assists in supporting the consciousness in feeling – feeling what love feels like in the physical body. This brings it into actuality rather than the smaller frequency band-width of duality. In duality, we have pain, suffering, disease, and separation, and its opposite becomes a concept of what love is. You are increasing your frequency bandwidth when you <u>actually</u>

*feel love – the Creative Force – in your body, which transcends
duality and unifies.*

For now, it seems the masks are still in the majority – agreeing to the conditioning that this is real and this is life. But I know that this cycle of darkness is over. The Field of Source Light is present, which dissolves any limiting matrix or structures that heretofore seemed so real. We know this through the larger-cycle shift that the ancient Native peoples foretold and through the whole perceptions of those who have been activated within. It may still appear to be chaotic, but what we see in our outer world now, in the form of what remains with confused governmental leadership, along with the obvious pain and suffering in our world, is simply the auto-spin cycle of our own unconscious deference to the dying matrix. And while we all love our technology, the distractions of such can postpone or even thwart our own awakening into what is natural and true. Unless we have a moment like Louis C.K., interrupting the loop to notice a real feeling, then we may never find the restart button and initiate our whole and natural state again – which is truly the access point to the greatest technology we can imagine – our own bodies.

Again, it might be wise to question the obvious rush to implement artificial intelligence through transhumanist technologies when clearly we haven't even tapped into the larger percentage of our own, real, Source-infused intelligence. And by not fully activating, owning, and filling in the rest of the story through the feeling, feminine, spherical resonance, it causes us to continue seeking solutions *out there.* Instead, we are in a position now to wholly recall that every bit of value and intelligence is already within, waiting for us to recognize it beneath the old programming.

Verbal Transmission: June 23, 2006

*It is a big assignment to choose to invite this experience within the
Western culture, for the way you have designed your lives is one*

of distraction, to say the least. Your flurries of activity and your busy lives assuredly prevent this connection with the Oversoul. Yet, if there is a desire for the infusion, for the memory of your total identity, then it will be so. But you must not concern yourself with timelines, do you see? Should you be desirous of the reconnection, the remembrance of your totality, then a discipline of intention is advised. This may come in many, many, many forms. Move in the direction that you are drawn. In discipline, what is meant from this view, is not so much existing rituals, for truly the creation of your own physical rituals would be more powerful at this time. By discipline, what is meant here is that in your practice, you are restating your intention to know, to be alive, and to be present. This may take the form of moving meditation or still meditation. It may take the form of physical exercise. It may take the form of mantras, chanting, or toning, and it may take other forms that humans are introducing now into your realm. It matters not, as long as the form feels comfortable to you. With each disciplined practice, voicing your intentions is advised. What do you want? There must be a container of intention. There must be the invitation for this transformational experience to occur in your lives.

Now, the big question that has rung out into the ethers from planet Earth is, where will I find the time to do that? Simple. Where you begin is right where you are. Are you busy in your office and recognize that it is not fulfilling to you? Then you begin there. Take a moment for yourself, whether it is at your place of work or when you arrive at home. Close the door. Be alone. Lock it if you must. And say out loud,

"I choose to be fulfilled in this life. I welcome this. I know that there is more to who I am, and I invite this loving being into my life here and now. I am willing for my life to change benevolently for

me and for those around me in order to achieve this balance, this peace, that I know is possible."

Do you see what we are saying about beginning right where you are? There is the perception that you have your work life, you have your home life, you have your recreational life, and you have your spiritual life. There are so many categories of human now, that you do not allow yourself to be your spiritual self at work or your recreational self with your spiritual self and so on. You intend to fuse all of these benevolent qualities of yourself. That is the whole idea! So begin right where you are, for that is where the present moment is accessed, and this is where enlightenment flows through – into the present moment. There is no reason anymore, at this point now in time, for humans to procrastinate. And why would you choose to procrastinate the fullness, the wisdom, the skills, and the talents that are yours? The reasons that we perceive that procrastination could occur is the fear of your world and your life [as you've known it] falling apart. Know that the parts that no longer serve you and those around you will fall away – fall apart and fall away. But wouldn't that be part of your intention anyway?

Transformation is occurring at this time in your evolution, whether you consciously choose to participate or not. The joy, the ecstasy, and the fulfillment are available to humans right now. Many of you have already experienced this, or tastes of it, as you say. It is being done. It is being demonstrated. And you will see evidence of this in the coming years on your planet. An explosion of consciousness, an explosion of awareness, an explosion of joy – a renaissance like none other will be witnessed on your planet. Invite it now. There is no more waiting. So in this way, enlightenment is not the last step on your path of evolution. It is the beginning.

As consciousness develops, the body will act as a donkey for only so long. Men as much as women need to know that their soul is grounded in their own loving matter. "This is who I am. Every cell in my body tells me this is of value to me – not to my persona, to me." That is the container whose feeling can be trusted because it is grounded in reality.[22]

\- DR. MARION WOODMAN

XII

A Treasure Worth the Dive
Finding the Courage to Go Deep

———⟡———

Just one wave is all it takes
To recall my ocean song
Sing along, sing along, sing along
It's here
No fear
Begin to swim
Begin by diving in [23]

~ E. MEYER (LYRICS)

Somewhere in the mid-forties range in my life, I became ultra-aware that it would be irresponsible to fling any more muddled and unconscious feelings onto another human being, otherwise known as e-motions – in this case, unconscious energies in motion. It seems I was being shown in this lucid approach that it was my responsibility to dig the buried feelings up and out for my own conscious review and release – before they could be triggered and projected out onto others. I never felt alone with this process, though. The Presence seemed ready and willing to hold the space, almost as if it has always been here, waiting for the opportunity to fill in and become the space when that crazy hoarder of buried trauma gave notice and moved out.

I learned that through my own restoration of life force energy, and awareness of my own growing honesty-resonance, my eventual response-ability to my tribe (or community) would be to express only conscious, authentic feelings from this balanced and actual place of Love. I could not expect anyone out there to heal what I alone had chosen to shove in the underground of my consciousness. After all, it happened on my watch and in my individual consciousness. Even though it was easy to get caught up in the oppressive mass conditioning to disown and bury it, I could blame no one "out there" for ultimately killing my authentic self or for my choice to replace it with a substitute, symbolic identity in the world.

I made some modifications to the resonance exercises, as suggested by the Intelligence, to eliminate nouns and pronouns from my expressed feelings. That part made sense to me. As I understood it, essentially anything "out there" that I might plaster my feelings on – aka disown, blame others for, or engage in analysis from an intellectual front – was not a fully owned feeling of mine. It went on and on. I continued to be prodded with the same question, "What are you feeling now?" Each time I dug a little deeper, and when I did, I began to shake and feel far more vulnerable and exposed. Naturally, I was beginning to uncover and give voice to hidden or masked feelings – feelings that had never, ever been voiced aloud. It was fascinating to reach a place of shame and embarrassment for the expression of my own honest feelings – even when I knew that absolutely no one else could hear!

These were taboo feelings that were highly classified – culturally, religiously, politically, sexually, and so forth. In the early 1990s, I worked with secret and top secret data behind ironclad walls, floors, and ceilings – a perfect metaphor for what I had designated as personally classified, need-to-know data within my own consciousness. Except in this case, the need-to-know from within me or from anyone around me had been eliminated through conditioning. We all agreed to keep our truth SECRET, and to guard it accordingly. But in my case, these walls were breached – by frequency and by a universal energy that proved to me that under no circumstances can our consciousness be limited or contained. Rather, beneath all that has been kept secret and wrapped in shame, we naturally carry the Vibrational Truth of this buried treasure – Source.

> *The most important things are the hardest to say. They are the things you get ashamed of, because words diminish them – words shrink things that seemed limitless when they were in your head to no more than living size when they're brought out. But it's more than that, isn't it? The most important things lie too close to wherever your secret heart is buried, like landmarks to a treasure. And you may make revelations that cost you dearly only to have people look at you in a funny way, not understanding what you've said at all, or why you thought it was so important that you almost cried while you were saying it.*

~ Stephen King

I took it as far as I possibly could, until I couldn't find any other feeling hiding in the dark corners and crevasses of my personal, dungeon. After being expressed, each feeling would lead to another – and another and another. When and where did we bury these unwelcome feelings? Is it the subconscious? Unconscious? The underworld? Thankfully, we don't need a label to uncover these trapped bubbles of life force energy. The closer I got to digging the feelings out (and sending them out through my throat, in the closest match of felt sense to words), the more it brought my heart and body humming back to life. I could feel a primal rumble, as well as a light exploding in every cell of my body – not unlike the Koyopa-Kundalini experiences I'd been consumed with in the past. Except this method was far more conscious and methodical, and I was fully empowered to take the lead in this loosely choreographed dance with Source. Together we were healing, transforming, and transcending all that was not aligned with Truth.

After some time, I came to a point where my process seemed to slow down. I talked out a feeling when it arrived, but at this stage, they were emptying quickly, and I realized that more and more, the magnetic force had begun filling the empty crucible within – to the point that I was vibrating so strongly, I could no longer speak. The last thought I had before I felt that I should turn on the record button was, "Hey, this is exactly the feeling I had as a child! I would sing and then I would land on a note... and... and..."

Boom! I had no body, no voice, and no thought. I landed in pure resonance and absolute oneness... again. My consciousness had no "Eileen" point of view. Yet it wasn't too long after, that I became aware of my actual voice speaking out loud,

*Knowing what you feel leads to feeling and restoring
what you've un-known.*

Hours later, following my anchoring back into local consciousness, I recorded the experience in my journal.

Journal Entry: July 25, 2006

The love conveyed here and the support filled me beyond words, and I wept. I found myself in a multidimensional grid that was presented in a spherical, globe-like structure. It was infinite yet presented in this resonant and round feeling. The light surrounded me, and I felt enormous love and heat coming from ALL. I was completely included and at home in this grid... equal in all respects.

It was me, yet it wasn't the me that I had once thought I was. I became aware that my hands moved from my heart to form a variety of different hand gestures and back again, synchronized with beautiful, foreign-sounding words pouring effortlessly out of my mouth. I remembered that this had happened off and on my whole life – waking up in the night, completely enveloped in the sweetest love imaginable, with these "light words," along with my hands moving, or dancing, magically on their own.

It was through my honesty and innocence – speaking it out loud directly, courageously, forcefully, and fearlessly – that initiated heart resonance. Because I have directly experienced it many times over, I have no remaining hierarchical experience of Life on Earth or Beyond. I know this Love as myself. This is the Light. This is the Way. And in Christian terms, could this be what was referred to as the return of Christ or Christ consciousness in these times? What if it isn't a robed man descending from the clouds but rather the activation, the inheritance, and the full embodiment of these de-conditioned missing pieces of our Selves? And obviously, this is not "new" material. What is new though, is perception. A whole new perception can transform everything.

I refuse to believe that we are victims of our individual or worldly conditioning. It's why I have laid out my personal life experience in the pages of this book – from innocence, to victim, to transformation, and a return to innocence again. I have directly experienced Source Love, and it wholly changed me. I am aware of my human experience as well as my universal oneness with Source, and I am aware that every human being arrives with this treasure at their core. My entire life has been a gradual adaptation to the eternal Song of the Universe – merging it with my local consciousness on Earth, and quite frankly, trying not to go insane as I went through the cycles of remembering, forgetting, and remembering again. For so many years, it felt as if an "other" consciousness was "visiting" me. Indeed, it also felt like the More, or Whole, of my consciousness had reached through the container, and like a blow gun, it shot this Love and Life directly into my cells: "Wake up. It's time. Remember who you are!"

Together we have individually and collectively arrived in the foyer of greater consciousness. However, not all will choose to expand. Those who have awakened will find that compassion is naturally present when necessary. We forgive – not only for the stops and starts of our own everyday practice of wholeness, but also for other humans who seem to be completely unaware of their Creator-given capacity for wholeness. We become ultra-aware that they are trapped in fear, living the stories of the past, completely identified with their worldly character(s) and completely conditioned to believe that this is all there is. In fact, for some there may never be self-reflection or a question of, "Could this be all there is?" Remember, this is what we once referred to as a "normal" human: one who would describe himself as "happy, for the most part." I can forgive his forgetfulness and the angry words and actions that can arise from the unconscious pain, misunderstanding, and confusion that are still covering over the deeper treasure within. Why? Because I continue to witness, forgive, and heal my own misunderstandings. There is always something deeper, or with ever-widening context, to rediscover.

Many of us have been in a perpetual state of curiosity, content to read about others' experiences in books or go to hear them lecture because it's smart, fun, stimulating, and inspiring for a while. But in the past, the individual choice to truly know, and to directly inquire into one's own wholeness, rarely occurred. You can directly know your Source-Creator through a Field of Love right now. Why is this not as interesting as looping in the program of exploring vicariously through others? Sadly, I found that many do not respond enthusiastically, and if they do, they are unable to sustain it. Why is that?

My sense, and what has been reinforced through the translations, is that in order to break this spell we must individually arrive in our own experience of resonant Oneness with Source. But we should also recognize that even though we might have established this actual, feeling marker within our bodies, we may still have a tendency to become afraid again – especially when we feel that we are alone and that no other human is standing with us or mirroring this truth in our day-to-day lives. Instead, we may feel isolated and become terrified when, in our daily practice of truth and honesty, we continue to hear only the timid echoes of our own voice. We may decide that we can't seem to nurture and grow it on our own or within our conditioned communities, so we fall back into duality, and the upside-down collective consciousness of the world. All the while we have the awareness of this Truth knowing now, and in the past when we became aware of the larger aspects of ourselves that are "too bright" and unwelcome here, we tried to stuff or hide it back in the underworld. It won't work this time.

> *Neither do men light a candle, and put it under a bushel,*
> *but on a candlestick; and it giveth light unto all that are in*
> *the house. Let your light so shine before men, that they may*
> *see your good works, and glorify your Father*
> *which is in heaven.*

~ MATTHEW, 5:15 AND 5:16
KING JAMES BIBLE

It is unhealthy to hide the treasure and inheritance that one has rediscovered within. In the beginning, it takes great courage to bring this through. For all of you who are on an active path of actualizing or awakening now, it's time to be bold – far more bold than you ever could've imagined you'd be. We are a choir and a community of those who have been hearing, singing, and strengthening the Universal Song. Let us stand in oneness and raise our voices loudly, harmonically, and valiantly. And let us demonstrate the sovereign platform and power of our own wholeness, as we consciously cocreate a Whole, New Earth.

Verbal Transmission: September 11, 2007

You are being encouraged to let go the last of your attachments to personality and self, and yes, this does feel like death. Yet, this is what you want and have been asking for. This is what many ask for, but they have no idea, no sense, of what they are truly asking for. When it gets down to it, even though the words are present, the willingness goes out the window when there is a threat to identity, to the conditioned identity that has been created to live in the existing human world.

People say that they want to transcend, that they want to meet and know God, and when this Source energy begins to rattle around in their consciousness, the fear erupts, for there is no identification with this frequency. There is a loss of memory, for they have been invested for so long, for so many cycles, in the conditioned human world – this disconnected state from the rest of themselves. So there is the fear that erupts and is identified as the angry God or the devil character.

Therefore, the physical dying was the only solution that you have developed as a human race in order to actually reconnect with this Love, with this Universal Presence. This is the cycle that is ending. And in the process to stay in form and rejoin with Creation – with the Universal – there is a complete loss of identity, a complete surrender, as you say, to allow the form to be governed by the Universal Self. It does not mean that all relationships perish – all of your persons, places, and things – never to be seen again. It is then that that you press the restart button, and from that point forward, you are relating in actuality with others, rather than relating to an image that you have designed within this human construct.

Why would one want to resist becoming Universal? There is no marker, there is no book, and there is no story on your planet that prepares one for the actual meeting of the Un-known. Therefore, it is feared and resisted. And even those who have been preparing for years to allow this transformation, the full reversal, from separation to universal – even these people – experience resistance in the end, for they have had only glimpses of it. The primary foundation of their lives, in order to keep consistency with those around them, was to be focused in the conditioned world with the memory [of their transcendent experience] and the understanding that this is not all there is. You see, they carry that knowing for a time. And you call these people "enlightened," by the way. They know, but they still primarily operate within the human construct. They might pass on what they learn – report on what they have learned of the more. But your next step in your evolution is to be that more in all ways – including in physicality, in relationship with the Earth, and in relationship actually.

The guidance at this time is to continue in these present-moment interactions, whether it is in words in this way, or in a strictly feeling experience of it, you will be guided through this process to actual demonstration as you have been requesting – to demonstrate the Universal on Earth – to be That Which You Are in form. In the past, this has been theory, strictly theory, for how many examples have you experienced of the Universal Consciousness awakened on Earth? You have your stories about those characters who achieved this in the past. This is not sufficient for you to make the transition yourself. We are speaking to humans in general, for you have your examples embedded in your story, icons, archetypes, but how often have you wondered? How often have you asked to become that which you have projected as beautiful, as loving, as powerful, as compassionate? That is the next leap for all of humanity, and the opportunity now is to achieve this consciousness while in form, while maintaining your physicality. It is possible. And the possibilities are growing due to the willingness of some humans on Earth to take this next step.

Your dramas that you are experiencing now on the various stages throughout your human world will dissolve, and there will be little memory of them when this choice is acted on – to become That Which You Are, Heaven on Earth as you say. So it is true that we have been coming through this channel with words. The words come through for you. There is still the reporter aspect of this human identity, the channel, to send out words to report on this process, for that is how humanity perceives and has decided collectively – that words are the way to understanding. There is another way to understanding, and it is pure knowing and pure feelings. It is instinct. There is no analysis. There is no theorizing. It is simply present because you have allowed it to be present by activating this knowing capacity within your physical bodies. You see, it is the physical body that assists you in this understanding, and this way of perceiving.

In these coming times, choices will be made as to how you want to relate to Creation. Creation is at your door and wants to know you, wants to be you. And if you are not able to open the door and allow this harmonic reconnection with the rest of your Selves, then you will transform in the ways that you have been conditioned – believing that you must lose the body in order to reconnect with Creation, with the rest of yourselves. It is as simple as that. So you have created the opportunity, collectively, to do this. Creation works this way. It is all play. It all comes from, "I wonder what would happen if we did it this way? What if we did that? What might that be like? Oh, let's find out!" And so here you are, finding out!

Any which way that you choose to redefine yourselves in a larger sense is a beautiful path in Creation. It is all included in Creation. It is all loved. It is all supported. For when you come back together to discuss and to explore what you have all learned, what you have all discovered about how it all works, there will be many voices, many views, and it is all shared within the circle of Universal Love. Even though it appears that there is darkness, it is but distorted Love.

It is as if you are children playing house out in the backyard. The time is coming when mother will holler out, "It's time to come home children. It's time to gather around the table. It's time to eat. It's time to take a bath. Playtime is over for now." Mother Earth is calling you back to the table, back to what is real, back to the truth of all that you are connected to. It may be fun to explore a variety of ideas and imaginings, but the calling to Home is occurring now. You have projected yourselves into an imaginary scenario, and that can only last for so long, for it is not based on what is whole and real. You might recall that as children, your imaginings took you to wonderful places, and sometimes not so wonderful places, but eventually your tummies signaled to you that you were hungry, or your eyelids became heavy. You were tired. The signals that it's time to come home are in your bodies. So your bodies pull you back from the images and walk you home – home to the mother, home to the father, home to the nurturing. Home.

The next day, after your rest, after your regrouping with the rest of your Self, you might go out to explore again and imagine and insert yourselves into many adventures, grand adventures. We will leave it at that, this metaphorical way of speaking, for it truly boils down now to your willingness to allow this transformation to occur. Many of you have been purifying in your own ways. You have created your own problems and challenges in order to assist you in the breaking down of the reality that you have become invested in. It is all breaking down now. It is breaking down so that you can establish your foothold with the Mother, and so *that you can be fed from this solid anchoring with Earth. You will understand more of your capacities and more of the possibilities once your feet land on the Earth as it actually exists. When you network back in with Creation in this way, you will know all that you need to know when you need to know it. And life as you know it and have known it will be completely transformed. Your Universal Identity will walk, speak, move, and have its whole being on Earth.*

Pray. Ask – if you wish to fulfill your original intention to walk as a Universal being on planet Earth. If you still intend this, awaken enough to pray, and say it out loud. Reestablish a conscious partnership with Creation, and you will be guided. You will have what you need – all ways. But there is the awakening, to a degree, that is required for you to ask, for you to state, that you remember the intention and you're ready to proceed in trust. As you let go of all that you have known, let go of the past, and allow the present fullness to occur.

For some, even the spiritual ones and the spiritual workers, it will be difficult to relinquish the image, the identity, that has been established, for it is where they perceive their worldly sustenance to come from. You see, whether you are a criminal or you perceive yourself as a spiritual worker, there is still, in many cases, the same degree of identification with something that has proved to be sustaining in their worldly lives.

There are some events that will shift, change, extinguish, or accelerate that which is currently in motion, currently being created by and from human identity. What is being created now from the person (or people) that you perceive yourself to be at this timing may not come to full fruition due to collective events – events that are set in motion by your collective guidance and partners with you in this collective creation. Mother

Earth is one partner. The Sun is another Partner. And the Moon is a partner for your experience on Earth. Some of these larger movements will occur due to previous agreements that it be so at this timing in order to achieve what you have all intended to achieve together.

There is nothing to fear. If there is one message that we could get through and have received by humans, it would be that there is nothing to fear.

Over the years, I have refined these exercises through my ongoing practice. While it has transformed me, and my entire life, there is no trumpet-sounding summation or final conclusion for you that will wrap this book up into a tidy closing ceremony. It is always a practice of Presence in each and every new moment.

There is a song, a long-forgotten song, that will fill in the blanks. But it is you who must provide the open air, the breezeway for the song to carry into your heart and every cell of your being. In the past, we were conditioned to seek and quickly find Love and Value in our human-made structures and in other conditioned people who existed "out there." I believe we have taken this experiment as far as we can go. When we allow the Song of Universal Resonance to fill us in, we seek nothing. But we fill up and out with so much joy and fulfillment that it seems all we are motivated to do is share this harmony and contribute to the benevolent transformation of our world.

A basic outline for activating heart resonance is provided next. Understand that it is difficult to break this practice down into linear steps (1-2-3) because it is deeply personal, and it becomes your own unique, choreographed dance with Source. It is important to trust in your own abilities to design and implement this, but only if you feel an attraction to it. Remember, you might discover a completely different pathway to wholeness. I am simply sharing portions of my map and travelogue. If it inspires, go for it. If not, I trust that you will discover the perfect road to wholeness in your own lives.

For those who resonate with these methods, my intent for the next phase is to begin facilitating groups to help guide you through this process and perhaps help you to feel something directly – something that you can use as a feeling baseline in your own future practice of Presence. Again, once the body feels the Source Frequencies again, it will not forget. In addition, being around others who are practicing the same reinforces our collective efforts and gives us permission to continue to value and expand into it until it is personally owned and embodied.

Activating Our Inner Tools of Resonance and Reconnection to Source

- *Seek out the methodologies* and people that will facilitate the healing of your traumas. I recommend EMDR and Brain-spotting, but there might be other methods that you are drawn to. You do not have to be a war veteran or have experienced violent trauma for these methods to help. We have all experienced trauma simply by being survivors of this fragmented, upside-down world.
- *Eat healthy, balanced foods* – organic if possible. While it's not always possible, I do my best to be mindful of this. Affordable organic food is increasing in availability. I have lived at or below poverty levels for many years of my life, and with strong intention, I have managed to consume mostly organic foods.
- *Exercise regularly* in ways that feel right and appropriate for your body. Breath and movement occurring in the natural world is preferred, but if this is not possible, move in the ways you are able.
- *Meditate.* You don't have to know how. If you have no idea where to begin, follow what others have demonstrated until you find

your own way. This can also be combined with the Feelings Aloud exercise (below). Be truthful and state your heart's intention to awaken and feel Source. The main point here is that you simply begin to be regularly present – with words out loud or not. Show up in pure innocence. Be raw. It's best to admit you know nothing than to bring past images of spirituality and ideas of sacredness into this exercise.

- **Plant Medicines**. If you feel inspired, and with the support of qualified facilitators, you may avail yourself of natural plant medicines to support your intention to release, heal, and restore your life and balance with Mother Earth. (Be fully aware of your own individual choices in relation to local and federal laws).

- **Feelings Aloud** (Allowed). Create private, dedicated times to speak out loud with full Honesty and Innocence. (Same time, same place if at all possible.)

  - Whenever you become aware of deeper discomforts, self-judgments, or even excuses as to why you shouldn't show up for this feeling meditation, always begin with the firm statement, "I am here." State it like you mean it. Feel that you are actually *here* in your body. Then begin answering the question, "What are you feeling?" Answer as honestly as possible in that moment. Include your body – without the person, place, and thing identifiers. Follow the threads of feeling. Should energy dissipate or you find yourself looping in thought, simply return to breath, state, "I am here," and answer the question again and again. Eventually, your body will tell you whether what you are saying out loud is actually true. Over time, you will learn what this genuine match or harmonic resonance inside your body feels like.

  - You will also learn what a purely mental statement feels like in your body. There is a disconnect. The words will come from past conditioning and aren't connected to anything authentic feeling, body based, or real.

- When you feel the resonant match of truth, it's as if you are starting a fire. Initially you sense a few slight sparks of connectivity, but until you really get the fire going – a perfect match of Presence, Innocence, and Truth – you'll just be talking about wanting to start a fire or reflecting on one of your past fires. The drama around past or future stories of fires don't count. Your attention must be in the present moment to feel the warmth, the light, and the resonant Source wisdom.

- What are you feeling now? Continue until you truthfully and consciously match the truth that sets you free. You will know it when it occurs. There is no guesswork. You are tuning your instrument. Your body will respond, and this will be your proof source.

- Incidentally, if you are in a crisis situation, it is also advised that you breathe deeply, and then strongly feel and state, "I am here." Say it out loud until you feel that you actually are *here*. The present moment is where you receive what you need to know at the moment you need it. Understand that God Source or angels or guides cannot hear you or find you if you are looping within the intellect. This includes the recitation of prayers too. Activate your heart and body. Feel and show that you mean it. This helps place you in the multidimensional, natural-network radar with your Source.

- ***Once you feel success*** with this, your inner guidance (which is in sync with your heart-body consciousness) will expand from a singular tone of energy to a sense of being filled in or being brought online with your greater frequency vibration or song. You could experience it as an inner dialog, instantaneous understandings (knowing), or simply the expansion of pure, loving heart resonance. Your continued practice and attention will guide you further into a felt-synchronization with your Source, or angels, or whatever you choose to name this Love in the moment.

I look forward to hearing how your own dance of honesty and innocence unfolds for you. Know that once you achieve the pure resonant state, the next stage is creating or manifesting. There are no steps for this practice, as this Source question will arise in the perfect timing within you, "What do you want?" Then begins the direct engagement, resonant dialog, and co-creation with your Source.

These exercises assist and support you at whatever level of heart or emotional awareness you have engaged so far. While it may seem that there are some humans who do not explore or cultivate anything other than the programmed mind and intellect, know that they too have a choice for Love in these times, and they might surprise you in the end. It may appear that some have successfully blocked out heart awareness to keep entrained within the smaller bandwidth of existence, but know that every human being, in any new moment, has the ability to come online with whole consciousness. All these natural technologies are available and within – every one. And as indicated in the previous outlined steps, once balance is achieved with resonant wholeness, creation and manifestation is the next phase – working with universal law and energy to restore and uplift all human life on Earth.

On the flip side, it is my understanding through these translations that should people refuse the opportunity to expand into the full power of their harmonic consciousness and capacities, they may continue to be very easily programmed. This has been a seductive system that has rewarded people with monetary resources and power for remaining within the contained mind. If we are unwilling to feel, we will be unable to expand into feeling and knowing the full sound of Source Love, and the abundance that is available to us throughout the natural, multidimensional network. So when you see what you once defined as leaders in your world – no longer embodying what you now know and define as true, representative leadership – have compassion for them. Help everyone in your community to understand and respect your choice for love – not so much in words alone, but in an outer demonstrable way. Allow people to choose as they will – Love or fear. This might be painful in some cases, as we may have considered those who choose fear to be dear friends and family members in the smaller context. But once you are connected and activated within heart consciousness, it is already known that life is eternal, and there will always be opportunities to make new choices.

Verbal Transmission: May 24, 2015

Many of you are thrilled that this timing is here, for you have known inherently that this is why you are here – to move through this expansion while in form. This is the fun of it. This is the joy of it. And you are here. What do you choose?

Now, we understand the fear around stepping into the unknown and feeling alone with this. Naturally, this is more frightening when you do not have a sense of your wholeness and connectedness to All. So in this now moment, you have the opportunity to speak your truth out loud and to connect with others in this conscious presence, and you have the opportunity to build teams to apply the feminine principles of community and cooperation – moving forward with this balance, this awareness, and this acceptance of the power and abilities and capacities that you have at your disposal. It is simply opening the toolbox and peering in, discovering what excites you, what you can envision for your life and your future, as well as what feels like past memories returning to say, "Remember when you were excited about this as a child? Remember that? When you felt so expanded?" These pieces return as well, and it strengthens you.

It will accelerate more rapidly – this opening into creation in these more expanded dimensional frequencies – if you practice speaking truthful feelings with each other in honesty and innocence. This will rapidly propel you into a more comfortable, joyful, and abundant life on Earth.

XIII

Humanity's Full-Circle Transformation
The New Children, Koyopa, and Adapting to Wholeness

———— ∞ ————

Koyopa (n) lightning [Momos]; inner soul
(receives supernatural messages)

LANGUAGE OF MAYAN K'ICHE'
TEACHINGS FROM THE MAYAN FIRE PATH, GUATEMALA

Since the approximate timing of 2012, the Mayan End of the Long
Count, the Galactic Center is sending wave upon wave and infinite
fields of "Good morning. Wake up!" messages to you. For those who still
feel that they are waiting for something to happen *out there*, know that
there is absolutely nothing to wait for anymore. No one is coming to save
you from what many of us feel is a strange and painful reality. *You* are the
director. *You* are the savior. *You* carry this wisdom in your DNA and in
every cell of your body. Activate it, reconnect, and radically transform your
reality. On the other hand, if you have found a sense of belonging and balance in the world as you have come to know it, then I congratulate you and
I wish you much joy and fulfillment in your future experience on Earth.

These new galactic frequencies are pure Love with pure loving intent.
The vibrational messages are pressing into our hearts now, and once we
consciously clear and open the doorways to Home, the energies do not

need to be translated into words for us to benefit from the nourishment of this long-awaited food. As we come online again, it feeds and informs us that it's possible to fully ignite who we are now through a strengthening network of a heart-based, cosmic consciousness that validates and supports us in what we always knew inside: we not only belong to something more, we *are* more.

Much to my great relief, I found the messages from these Visitors to be demonstrable and true. I learned that the practice of present-moment innocence and truth telling activates the body's memory of the language of harmonic resonance. It awakens us to our greater capacities as well as an undeniable, felt interconnectivity with the natural world, our natural human family, and all our cosmic relations.

Indeed, we have been taught that the unknown is frightening, but soon enough, we may have the actual experience and feeling of being backed into that proverbial corner of, "Do I stay with the increasing confusion, pain, fear, abuse, and limitation of what I know? Or am I willing to know thy Self, trust as the little child again, and leap into the expansive unknown?" Feel free to be inspired by my story, or the stories of others who are remembering and simultaneously reorienting to their unique signature tone – rejoining the Symphony of the Universal, the Whole, the Awake.

I have been informed by this Intelligence, repeatedly throughout my life, that there are far more of us awakening here than we consciously realize. I am convinced it's because each one has believed him- or herself to be alone with it. The fear of fully being who we are, or actualizing ourselves, has kept a lid on it – literally. Because we have lived and transcended these repeated experiences of paradox and we have not only survived but have embodied more of our natural state on Earth, the potential to become demonstrators and community builders on this solid platform of Truth is positively infinite. The greatest game changer of all is when the awakened externalize this practice of Presence and Truth and freely share the growing spectrum of humanity's multidimensional gifts and capacities – from the ground up.

I hear so many people say, "I want this awakening! I know this is true!" And I respond, "Wonderful! Gather your courage, speak this intention aloud, and begin to demonstrate it." This is an evolutionary initiation. We are growing up – taking responsibility and action from a whole-hearted consciousness. It is literally how our individual and collective worlds are changed, as we willingly transcend the fragmented, repetitive, and restrictive loops of the past.

No person, place, or thing from this world can hand this to you. Others may inspire, but it is your heart only that ultimately says yes to the healing of all the foundational lies and related wounding of the past. This is our first step – a full commitment to *know* what we feel (local consciousness) in order to *feel* what we have Un-known (non-local consciousness) – until we wholly embody our multidimensional Selves. I was inspired by many people in my life, and for that I am eternally grateful. However, I did not discover these truths through reading or hearing someone else's interpretation of it. I was shown that the fullness of our Universal purpose and capacities are unlocked within – in the present – through the pure honesty and innocence of our hearts.

> *And Jesus called a little child unto him, and set him in the midst of them, And said, Verily I say unto you, Except ye be converted, and become as little children, ye shall not enter into the kingdom of heaven. Whosoever therefore shall humble himself as this little child, the same is greatest in the kingdom of heaven.*

MATTHEW: 2-4, KING JAMES BIBLE

It seemed that many scholars, scientists, and researchers weren't clear why the Mayan calendar dropped us off at December 21, 2012 – the Zero Point – with no further pageantry or clues as to what might come next. As a result, many decided or translated that the 2012 marker pointed literally to a massive cosmic-scale ending. December 21, 2012, came and went. The calendar did not end nor did the world. It continues just as it always has. This is indication enough for me that we are perched on an equally vast cosmic-scale beginning.

> *As for the Maya, they too were tracking precession as the basis of their World Age doctrine, but they were concerned with a completely different astronomical alignment, the solstice-Galaxy conjunction of A.D. 2012. They used the Long Count calendar (rather than the Calendar Round) to track this precessional alignment, which they calculated to occur on the Long Count date 13.0.0.0.0 [December 21st, 2012]. The Mayas' World Age cosmology concerned itself with a rare and profound galactic synchronization of our Earth-sun system's solstice meridian with the larger galactic frame of time. This is the Zero Point of the Galactic Cycle of precession, an event that previously occurred 26,000 years ago. The early Maya skywatchers understood this vast time cycle and brilliantly devised the Long Count calendar to end precisely on the Galactic Zero Point.* [24]

~ JOHN MAJOR JENKINS

Celebrated author, John Major Jenkins, refers to Mexico's pyramid of Chichen Itza as the site of an incredible mytho-cosmic story set in stone – and that the pyramid itself is a World Age calendar that points to this unique alignment in the Great Cycle of precession. Personally, I have only watched this incredible spring equinox event on television, and I heard it second-hand from friends who were present to perform or witness the ceremony on this celebrated date. On this enchanting day, the serpent-Kukulkan manifests in shadow play and slithers down the stairs, tail up in the air, heading toward the cenote (reservoir), and then is gone.

Jenkins adds his own understanding that Kukulcan's rattle is "centered in the Pleiades and the serpent manifestation is literally the pointer to a zenith conjunction of the sun and the Pleiades. And it may in fact herald the fabled 'return of Quetzalcoatl' (Aztec) or from the Maya's perspective, the 'return of Kukulkan.' [25]

> *The Citizens of ninth-century Chichen Itza believed their*
> *city would be bathed by the light of the great alignment*
> *sometime in the remote future. As such, the visible equinox*
> *manifestation seems to be a perennial clue to help those who*
> *are alive during the Maya end-times to get the message. The*
> *complete message. And the complete message appears to be*
> *that when the sun and the Pleiades join forces in the Heart*
> *of Heaven, Quetzalcoatl (Kukulkan) will return, and a new*
> *era will dawn.* [24]

~ JOHN MAJOR JENKINS

I believe the Maya knew that the Great Alignment in the stars would be mirrored within – as above, so below – the Heart of Heaven and the Heart of Earth. The Maya placed the rattle in the Pleiades, and the head of the serpent at the bottom of the pyramid's steps. As it descends, slithering down to the foot of the pyramid and disappears, we can begin to *feel* the message: The alignment is not just a heavenly one above. It is occurring here on Earth, within our hearts, and within our purified bodies. This is the prophesied return of the Plumed Serpent – quite literally meeting us at our very own feet, waiting for the Koyopa invitation to rise and ignite the totality of consciousness – in our physicality, on Earth.

In my experience, instead of being informed by the past, we can open and initiate our hearts and heart communion in the Great Alignment of the Present. Once aligned, we discover that consciousness is not linear, but rather spherical in nature. What we learn from both Kundalini and

Koyopa ancient symbols and descriptions is the activation of the serpent within has the power to initiate us into wholeness once again. By marrying both sides of the brain, the masculine and the feminine, and with the engaged presence and embodiment of the inner soul, we begin receiving, perceiving, and sharing information in wholly new ways.

However, it's important for me to note that while grateful for the data that I reference from these passionate and devoted authors, it takes a dedicated effort for me to read, compare, and note these markers from others, as my understanding is purely experiential, and my conclusions are based on instinctual, resonant data. I am simply pointing to the resonant markers that exist "out there" – the ones I so desperately sought throughout my life for the purpose of better describing and communicating with you. I offer these comparisons here so that I might provide additional framing for the reader or listener. Still, I encourage you to do your own research, in whatever materials you are drawn to. There are so many great resources on the topic – too many to count – in not only the Mayan Cosmology but also many others around the world that point to this awakening time on Earth.

However, I ask you to consider that for those who have had this direct experience, there is no need for this three-dimensional, historical proof source. It's interesting in context of our lives lived thus far, and for outer-world validation, but it's unnecessary to translate the resonant data. It's far more exciting to move forward in the grounded play and practice of wholeness. It's like forcing a child who has been waiting years for the monumental gift of a bicycle on Christmas Day to fully arrest the excitement in body and heart – and wait. Wait while "educated" men pontificate on the known history and mechanics of bicycles before the child can just jump on, take off, and directly experience the joy of riding it.

Koyopa has been translated as the "bolt, sheet, or body lightning" that occurs within our own physical bodies. In my experience, it is the individual human being – body, mind, spirit – making love with the cosmos and allowing the ecstasy to culminate into the embodiment of the inner soul. It is the "path of the Feathered Serpent" and the return of the feminine.

I believe the Maya (and others) knew that it would be arriving within us – restoring the marriage of the masculine and feminine within, and, in essence, bringing our whole consciousness back online. It appears that they trusted in our physical and spiritual potential to discover this for ourselves.

Both Eduardo and I discovered this Mayan word (Koyopa) and meaning recently, on the precise Mayan Calendar Day of Kan or Chiccan (the serpent) on November 15, 2016. Even after years of full immersion into the study and unraveling of the Mayan Wisdom, only now we discover this term in our notes and lessons from Guatemala over fifteen years ago – dropped into our awareness, like a gift to be opened in perfect timing. It truly weaves it all together, and for me personally, it helps to clarify what I have spent a lifetime desperately trying to explain without words. Sure, the word "Kundalini" was available to me, and I still use it from time to time to help translate, but the actual experience I had did not resonantly match its over-marketed use in America. It felt to me that the term had already been undermined to such a degree that the true meaning and experience was nearly lost on the Western mind. Therefore, I was more excited to unearth and employ the new-ancient word, Koyopa.

This opening in my body and consciousness did not occur over my lifetime because I am somehow special or different. The experience of Koyopa is for humanity. It opens the heart of Heaven, the Heart of Earth, and the Heart of Humanity, and once restored, we naturally commune and receive the supernatural messages from our Source and so much more of our Universal nature that has yet to be coaxed into language.

Many of our great teachers and the wisdom of the ancients pointed to this same Truth – that is, in Christian terms, "the Kingdom of Heaven is within." In Mayan terms, "Koyopa" introduces us to our cosmic, core, universal identity – directly. After all, the Mayan Calendar provided very clear indicators as to the importance of our recent arrival in the calendar year 2012. It appears we have come full circle – 26,000 years full circle. While Hollywood had other, more profitable and frightening portrayals for this cosmic-cycle event, it truly marks the end of a 26,000-year galactic cycle – noted by the Maya as an emergence from darkness and disconnectedness into the full light of our infinite possibilities. The Maya, and other great civilizations from around the world, left behind ancient wisdom-stone messages and artifacts. They knew that we contained all that we required to receive the message within, wake up, and remember our natural design.

Certainly there are many pathways to waking up or snapping out of the unconscious routines we once considered to be life. You may have noticed some of the other messengers in our midst that are not so easy to ignore, as they too are right at our feet. The younger generations, and newly arriving children are showing us that they have an important role in this cosmic wakeup plan too.

> *Millennials don't want to be told what to do, how to believe,*
> *or how to do spirituality or anything else. So much of what*
> *millennials have been told is true about life hasn't worked*
> *out for them: their parent's marriages didn't last; the priest*
> *or minister was a sex offender or crook; the politicians were*
> *bought off by special interests; and corporations were greedy.*
> *(Yes, these are pejorative statements, but they represent a*
> *general impression of social phenomenon.) Because of this,*
> *millennials want to discover life on their own. Yet, they are*
> *open to learn from the authentic experience of others.* [26]

~ REV. LOUIS F. KAVAR, PHD

This is a whole new ballgame of backing the older generations into the proverbial corner. By the presence of these new children in our families and homes, we are pushed to examine more deeply our unconscious commitments to our past conformity and programming. It's not as easy to dismiss our own younger family members as crazy non-conformists, and abandon or "unfriend" them as we do others who have challenged our worldview. Remember, these younger generations are generally not able to lie or suppress authenticity as the older generations could. The young ones might try to appease you and your conditioned ways, but it isn't sustainable, and the eventual backlash could become quite uncomfortable in the end. They will be who they are.

Which system serves and sustains you, your families, and the planet more wholly and efficiently? The known, limited one that we agreed to in the past that is crashing down before our very eyes? Or the benevolent unknown that is expanding within human hearts now? I know what the new children choose. It's crucial that we realize the importance of their gifts now, and it's even more important that we appreciate the love and courage that it takes to arrive in these evolutionary windows of time as disruptors to our outdated beliefs, platforms, and ideas. If we support them in achieving their full and balanced potential, their vibrational presence alone is likened to the strike of a cosmic tuning fork, whereby we are called to let go of the past conditioning that no longer rings true, rise out of fragmented consciousness, and begin to trust in our harmonic experience of wholeness.

Verbal Transmission: October 14, 2005, New Children

The energetics to support these new beings, the food you might say, is available to them if they are supported in being who they are. Now, you see, these new children are not able so much to project mentally. They are unable to create an image and live from that place. They will die. It is not possible.

Therefore, it is most crucial – and these children are counting on you, the adults – to invite the truth of your being, to invite the realignment of your being, to release all the fears and the misunderstandings that block you from full alignment. These are fears and past traumas. These are beliefs that have been acquired and are more of a collective conditioning. These are personal beliefs [as well] that have been acquired and thrown into the buffering area that keep you from the truth of yourself, that keep you distracted to the outer image. The energetics now on this planet are demanding more and more that the personal issues be resolved. Another way to put this would be that the energetics are supporting humans in becoming whole once again.

From the human's perspective, this will feel like a demand when frequencies are accelerated. The natural world is vibrating in a way that strongly invites humans to clear the way for their own natural Self to emerge into consciousness and to live the life here. This is what will help the children to more firmly plant themselves here on Earth and to do what they came to do. And that is to rebuild – not only with consciousness here, weaving back together all of who you are, but they will also be splendid examples of what this looks like, along with some of your pioneering adults. They are the way showers for those who need clear and concise examples. Also, these new beings will be involved, and very passionate I might add, about rebuilding the outer world and reestablishing the natural ways that work in this world – the ways that are in balance with Mother Earth.

Now, as indicated, these children must be supported for being who they are. And some of these parents now are seeing them and inviting them to be their natural selves. This is good, and there is more support and more awareness required; more consciousness-raising around these ideas is to come. Truly it is the balancing that is being called for within the adults that will lift these children to their rightful place in the world. It is the balancing within human consciousness on Earth that has the most direct effect on these children and their well-being. So it seems that it always comes back to the individual work – clearing the way for the natural Self to live in this world. Then watch the children rise up and bloom – blossoms everywhere that invite joy, that invite play, that invite passion and excitement for life itself, stimulating this entire world to step into the fullness!

Verbal Transmission: October 6, 2013, More on the New Children

Most humans live their entire lives in this existing landscape – filled completely with ideas, with concepts, and learning only to iden- tify with what exists, what they have known from the past. They are repeating and perpetuating, for there has been nothing to compare to except within your bubble, constantly making com- parisons from within the known.

Things are changing, as you say. In a way, you are all begin- ning to experience more of what your labeled autistic children ex- perience in their reality here at this timing on earth. They are born here and have intended not to identify with what is known, what has come before, what the collective has agreed to. Their intention is to allow more of the spaces so that they can be of assistance in helping the collective step into greater landscapes of conscious- ness. They come to individual families for individual and famil- ial intention as well as being part of moving the collective – the larger collection of humanity – into this direction of letting go of what you have always identified with as "real." It is a more gentle process for the families with autistic children to guide them into seeing and feeling a world where there is not so many spaces be- ing filled in with how it works or how it's supposed to be.

If you will note with these autistic children, they are always questioning, "Why?" "Why do you choose to do it that way?" Or quite often, what you say does not make sense to them. Obviously, we are speaking of the children, the beings, who are able to speak and articulate. There are some in this range of consciousness, in this particular intention, that hold this space and help move along the collective without the verbal connec- tion. Their work is somewhat deeper and more expansive and more misunderstood at this timing. Although, as you like to say, you are catching on. What you have labeled autism is more of a rooted spiritual movement in consciousness – souls who have had very specific intentions to move, or evolve, the consciousness along.

There is a choice that is being made within each individual at this time. Those who are attached through the glue of fear will stay with that glue. Those who have invested their attention, who have chosen to explore, to step into the unknown, and to welcome entirely new or different ways of perceiving will experience more and more expansion. And these beings will be learning, if you will, how to be actual, how to live fully present, how to stream more of their consciousness into an experience with Earth.

There are many, many old stories that so many of you are involved in telling and repeating. We are saying at this time that the stories will go. The stories are no longer relevant, for they are created from this world that you have always known.

You will not trade your old stories in for new stories. You will be actual.

Learn to let go of the old stories. Recognize the difference between fear and love, as we have given before. And be willing to step into open spaces where you initially do not have anything to identify with or relate to. Become comfortable with these feelings and more understanding will come. And understand that it will more than likely not look like anything that you are familiar with, that you can identify with from everything that has come before – everything that you have known. Do you understand? Be willing to feel and be with nothing and everything. Be comfortable with this. Practice this.

There is much more that we can share on these topics, for this is truly the crucible now. You are in it, and you are making this evolutionary leap in consciousness.

In conclusion, following my full disclosure of a life disrupted, I ask you: If you had lived a life like mine, what do you think you would've felt or done? How would you respond to full-body, spine-arching, initially terrifying energies? The shocking awareness of other beings and intelligence beyond our tiny world? Would you have allowed it to show you that we can make a conscious choice from fear to Love? That we are far more powerful than we were told? Would you have succeeded in demonizing or suppressing it? Would you have shared it with others? There are no right or wrong answers here.

I chose to integrate and share it. Sure, I continue to feel doubt around my abilities to fully understand these experiences, messages, and translations of frequency, but until we begin to truthfully communicate with each other – sharing these experiences and the data we receive from more expanded perceptions of reality – we will forever loop inside this extremely small reality. We must begin somewhere, and this book serves as a foundational cornerstone of my contribution.

Verbal Transmission: July 27, 2014

You have rediscovered other aspects of your identity – your universal or Source identity, if you will. Understand that the brain, the mind, and the intellect alone cannot process the fullness of your true identity – the fullness of what you are capable of.

Another way of being has been drummed into you, shall we say. It is a rhythm that sets the tone and the trance that you live within – the collective rhythm. And it has been demonstrated repeatedly for many of you that if you get out of that rhythm, then you stand out. The spotlight is on you – the crazy one – for feeling and experiencing something different from the program.

Now you do have the capacities to manifest fullness in your current form. This is not something that you then take and begin to process mentally to understand. So much of what we share and what we speak of is not intended to be processed or acted upon through your intellect. The interface that you have been taught to use in the trance, in the drumming of your collective encasement, is specific for your conditioning. Yet a blending is to occur. This is evolution – the larger aspects of Self communing with the more focused aspects of self.

I am not alone. There are many of us – born into this reality in the mid-nineteenth century and forward, to the newly arriving, more integrated children of today. For some of these contactees, or *experiencers of More*, within my generation, it seemed to be a lifelong plan of vibrational upgrades designed to remind the body and being that we are far more than our everyday thinking minds. I have been urged from within to give voice to this Universal Field of Love. The *ground troops*, or physical survivors of this dedicated expansion, are here not only to help and to reflect the knowing of what we are connected to but also to validate the children now. Together may we demonstrate the natural, the instinctual, and the infinite heart of humanity.

It's time to be bold. Let us have the courage to invite, reactivate rise, and ultimately shatter the lies. Without eyes to see and ears to hear, we believed unquestionably. The times for pretending to be blind, deaf, and dumb are old and done. We are not small. We are infinite. It's time to unleash the force of Truth and restore ourselves and the Earth to our natural states. This is what the Maya and ancient peoples held. I don't *believe* this because the suits and robes told me so. I know it because it's alive in my body and heart. This is the timing – the restoration and reorientation to the Source of All within.

This is my scratched-out roadmap, my life, my song. I believe that now is the time to lend an ear and a heart to experiencers of all kinds. We are travelers and researchers into the balance of our consciousness – the Heart.

We return with vital and urgent messages – to first admit our previous addiction to staying linear and small and then opening wide to the reintegration of the feminine. Feelings are absolutely key. It leads us directly to the sound and resonance of our Source. This is how we transform into our whole and natural state. This is how we transform the world.

I will no longer apologize for who I am, what I have recalled, and the ways in which I have recalled. In these volatile times, I highly recommend that you suspend your judgement of people like me, who have experienced more and who are courageous enough to share the truth of it with you. I believe much of humanity may now be backing itself into the proverbial corner, the corner that I and so many others have been backed into throughout our lives. It's a fork in the road where we must choose.

I ask you, who or what is crazier? Someone who shares a lifetime experience of meeting and learning the language of Source and otherworldly light beings, who has survived the massive, eye-opening activations within the physical body and resultant shifts in consciousness? Or is what we are now watching – our leaders, our wars, our sickness, our violence, our poverty – unfold in our communities and on television crazier? I believe that your greatest power and position in these times is that *you* get to choose your context now as well. Will you stay in the old, worn out, repetitive roadways of fear? Or are you willing to travel the undefined, unexplored, larger patterns of a huge Love that we were all conditioned to forget?

Nothing I share will fit into existing boxes here, but it doesn't mean that I, and so many experiencers, do not have great treasures to share – the most vital piece is the Love of the Great Mother. Unhealed trauma and the systematic disrespect and blocking of heart intelligence has created disconnected, terror-driven, highly manipulated human beings. This will not go on. Why? Because there is a long-forgotten fem-dragon coiled within every human being. She refuses to be contained in words, in the past, or buried deeply beneath our unhealed pain and shame. She is a fire that is awakening and restoring our bodies, our consciousness, our hearts, and all our relations – on Earth as it is in the Heavens.

Indeed, we are perched on the threshold of the greatest new beginning we can barely imagine.

Prepare yourselves. And let the Plumed Serpent rise.

We are the ones we've been waiting for...

HOPI ELDERS

Works Cited

1. **Forti, Dr. Kathy J.** The Sept 2015 Wave X Awakening. *Trinfinity8.* [Online] August 5, 2015. [Cited: October 15, 2016.] Ref: Dr. Peter Gariaev - Linguistic Wave Genetics. http://www.trinfinity8.com/the-sept-2015-wave-x-awakening/.

2. **Basheer, Dr. Fahad.** Heart Consciousness the Next Frontier in Brain and Neuroscience. *Waking Times.* [Online] April 6, 2016. [Cited: October 15, 2016.] Ref: Rollin McCraty, PhD, William A. Tiller, PhD, Mike Atkinson, Dr. Aju Rafeek. http://www.wakingtimes.com/2016/04/06/heart-consciousness-the-next-frontier-in-brain-and-neuroscience/.

3. **Sheldrake, Dr. Rupert.** *A Quest Beyond Limits of the Ordinary. Rupert Sheldrake and Bruce Lipton (97-min version).* Seattle, WA, USA : YouTube, August 1, 2012. References "The Hundredth Monkey" by Ken Keyes, Jr.

4. **Goswami, Dr. Amit.** *The Self-Aware Universe.* New York : Tarcher-Putnam Books, 1995.

5. *Eye Movement Desensitization: A New Treatment for Post-Traumatic Stress Disorder.* **Francine Shapiro, PhD.** s.l. : Journal of Behavior Therapy and Experimental Psychiatry, 1989, Vol. 20, pp. 211-217.

6. **David Grand, PhD.** What is Brainspotting? *Brainspotting.pro.* [Online] January 1, 2003. [Cited: January 10, 2017.] https://brainspotting.pro/page/what-brainspotting.

7. **Francine Shapiro, PhD.** What is EMDR. *EMDR.com.* [Online] January 1, 2016. [Cited: January 10, 2017.] https://www.emdr.com/what-is-emdr/.

8. **McKenna, Terence.** Jacques Vallee, Terrence McKenna, John Mack, Budd Hopkins on the Alien, UFO, Abduction phenomenon. *YouTube Johnny Tortuga.* [Online] January 15, 2014. [Cited: Feb 20, 2017.] As of February 2017, over fifty thousand views.. https://www.youtube.com/watch?feature=share&v=vB6uPBCVNPc&app=desktop

9. **Dictionary.com.** Dictionary.com. [Online] January 1, 2016. [Cited: January 10, 2017.] http://www.dictionary.com/browse/peak-experience?s=t.

10. **Gordon, Alan.** *My Heart Belongs to Me, Charlie Calello.* Los Angeles : s.n., January 1, 1977.

11. **Mack, Dr. John.** *Abduction: Human Encounters with Aliens.* New York : Scribner, 1994. pp. 258-259.

12. **Meyer, Eileen, [perf.].** To Free. Santa Fe : s.n., 2002.

13. **Rilke, Rainer Maria.** Duino Elegies by Rainer Maria Rilke. *Homestar. org.* [Online] January 1, 1992. [Cited: January 11, 2017.] Translated by Stephen Mitchell.

14. **Meyer, Eileen.** Inevitable. [prod.] Larry Mitchell. *Inevitable.* [Compact Disc] San Diego : Lightpaver Music, 1999. http://www.eileenmeyer.com/.

15. **Avila, Teresa of.** Teresa of Avila - On Those Words "I am for My Beloved". *Poetry-Chaikhana.* [Online] February 15, 2013. [Cited: January 11, 2017.] http://www.poetry-chaikhana.com/blog/2013/02/15/teresa-of-avila-on-those-words-i-am-for-my-beloved/.

16. **Meyer, Eileen Marie and The Modern Peasants, [perf.].** Descend on Me. [comps.] Eileen Marie Meyer. *The Modern Peasants.* San Diego : s.n., 1996.

17. **Richo, David.** *The Power of Coincidence.* Boston : Shambala, 2007.

18. **Meyer, Eileen, [perf.].** It's In You. [prod.] Larry Mitchell. *Songs of Anima.* Santa Fe : s.n., 2008. http://www.eileenmeyer.com/.

19. **Merculieff, Larry.** The Four Sacred Stone Tablets: Hopi and Tibetan Prophecy. *Red Ice Creations.* [Online] May 2, 2005. [Cited: January 12, 2017.] Addressing the Aleut Elders in Alaska - passing on the message of hope from the Hopi, Maori and the Stony Elders.

20. **Marion Woodman, Jill Mellick.** *Coming Home to Myself: Reflections for Nurturing a Woman's Body and Soul.* Berkeley : Conari Press, 1998. pp. 147-149.

21. **C.K., Louis.** Louis C.K. Hates Cell Phones. *YouTube Team Coco.* [Online] September 20, 2013. [Cited: November 13, 2016.] As of January 2017, over twelve million views.. https://www.youtube.com/watch?v=5HbYScltf1c.

22. **Woodman, Dr. Marion.** *The Ravaged Bridegroom: Masculinity in Women.* Toronto : Inner City Books, 1990. p. 181.

23. **Meyer, Eileen, [perf.].** Dive In. [prod.] Larry Mitchell. *Songs of Anima.* [CD] Santa Fe : s.n., 2008. URL: http://eileenmeyer.com.

24. **Jenkins, John Major.** *Maya Cosmogenesis 2012: The True Meaning of the Maya Calendar End Date.* Santa Fe : Bear & Company, 1998. p. 142.

25. —. *Maya Cosmogenesis: The True Meaning of the Maya Calendar End Date.* Santa Fe : Bear & Company, 1998. pp. 79-80.

26. **Rev Lou Kavar, PhD.** Millennials: Spirituality and Religion. *LouKavar. com.* [Online] October 2017, 2015. [Cited: January 9, 2017.] http:// blog.loukavar.com/2015/10/17/millennials-spirituality-and-religion/.

Links

Author-Musician-Experiencer, Eileen Meyer:
http://www.eileenmeyer.com/
https://www.facebook.com/KoyopaContactWithin/

Author-Channel-Mystic-Shaman, Robert Shapiro: http://benevolentmagic.
blogspot.com/

Author-Channel-Filmmaker: Darryl Anka: http://basharchanneledbydarry
lanka.org/

Artist-Producer, Larry Mitchell:
http://www.larrymitchell.com/

Psychotherapist, Candida Jones:
https://candidajonestherapist.wordpress.com/

Solace Crisis Treatment Center:
http://www.findsolace.org/

KBAC – Radio Free Santa Fe 98.1:
http://santafe.com/kbac/stream

FREE Experiencers – Resource for Experiencers of All Kinds:
https://www.facebook.com/groups/FREE.Experiencers/

About the Author

E ver since she can remember, Eileen Meyer felt that she was living two different lives – her normal outer life, and the inner one that could not be easily explained. Over the years she became accomplished in the areas of technical documentation, project-management, and all areas of digital media production, marketing, and related technologies. Her multimedia path was launched as a teenager when she was hired to work at the local production office for the movie-musical *Hair*. Later she learned to write, produce, and edit TV and radio ads, documentaries and instructional videos, and was employed as a voiceover artist for dozens of media projects.

Eileen loved to write her own stories and poetry from an early age, and while she would later become a blogger and publish articles in both print and online magazines, her main obsession as a child was to teach herself how to sing. And she did. Her singing career began in the late 1980's in Southern California, and ten years later she blossomed into an original singer-songwriter who wrote, recorded, and performed three solo albums. Her musical works have been licensed and used in a range of media productions – from Oprah's Oxygen Network to CBS Morning News, and numerous independent radio shows and documentaries.

All the while, her family, friends, and colleagues were mostly unaware that she was experiencing repeated contact in the form of angelic, interdimensional light beings and extraterrestrials. These types of visits simultaneously initiated powerful energetic episodes in her physical body – a transformative phenomenon known as Kundalini, or what the ancient Maya called *Koyopa*. Eileen simply knew it as energy, or a field of intelligent frequency that filled her body and sometimes differentiated into sound, light, foreign symbols, and streams of resonant, telepathic data. It took many years for her to navigate, adapt to, and integrate the experiences. Eventually she reached the epiphany that it was, in fact, a very real kind of contact that was reorienting her to a more holistic understanding of life. It also became clear that the high-vibrational energy itself was a feeling-language that could be translated.

Eileen also found a spiritual resonance with the teachings of the Maya, and in 2002, she walked the Mayan Fire Path and initiated in Tikal, Guatemala. Following these journeys and experiences, and three years of studying with Dr. Michael Mamas' School of Enlightenment and Healing, she knew without a doubt that her natural gifts were intuitive healing, empathic soul reading, and the translation of high-frequency intelligence into words and sound.

These repeated transformational episodes in Eileen's life radically changed her consciousness. She found herself becoming increasingly drained with the maintenance of two very different worlds – the limited one that most agree is "life," and the other more expanded world, as seen through a growing restoration of heart-brain or whole consciousness. Unfortunately, she found that sharing any of it with family or friends seemed to agitate them. It was easier to dismiss her as crazy, than to hear of her epiphanic experiences beyond the known world. Very few had a desire to venture beyond the existing "loops" of everyday human life to include the experiential, or anything other than what they'd been told. She learned that it was imperative to keep it to herself, as she could see that most were obsessively focused on making the highly-conditioned reality work. Eileen wanted an outer life that worked for her too, but found the existing scripts to be inadequate. It seemed that she already knew too much to pretend that there wasn't massively more to human consciousness. Thankfully, there were other humans who appeared along the way – ones who provided enough deep shamanic and soul mirroring so that she could feel a sense of nurturing, encouragement, and wholly belonging in the world.

Today Eileen is writing, talking and singing her story. She also shares the emotional-awareness tools that she translated from her visitors. Her evolving challenge is how to pour the invisible feminine wisdom into a linear-language format – to reach those who have unknowingly based their realities upon a mechanistic, fragmented model of life. The ever-present guidance throughout Eileen's life consistently shares that the "missing" feminine and spherical consciousness is being restored into humanity's body and awareness. And her entourage of angels, ETs, and frequency intelligence is reaching out to you with this encouraging message: Now is the time to break the spell of limitation, and to heal and reclaim the whole of your human design… then watch your outer world thrive.

For more information about Eileen's music and spiritual works, visit EileenMeyer.com.

CPSIA information can be obtained
at www.ICGtesting.com
Printed in the USA
FSHW022032080620
71026FS